Prehistory: A Very Short Introduction

VERY SHORT INTRODUCTIONS are for anyone wanting a stimulating and accessible way in to a new subject. They are written by experts, and have been published in more than 25 languages worldwide.

The series began in 1995, and now represents a wide variety of topics in history, philosophy, religion, science, and the humanities. Over the next few years it will grow to a library of around 200 volumes – a Very Short Introduction to everything from ancient Egypt and Indian philosophy to conceptual art and cosmology.

Very Short Introductions available now:

ANCIENT PHILOSOPHY
    Julia Annas
THE ANGLO-SAXON AGE
    John Blair
ANIMAL RIGHTS   David DeGrazia
ARCHAEOLOGY   Paul Bahn
ARCHITECTURE
    Andrew Ballantyne
ARISTOTLE   Jonathan Barnes
ART HISTORY   Dana Arnold
ART THEORY   Cynthia Freeland
THE HISTORY OF
    ASTRONOMY   Michael Hoskin
ATHEISM   Julian Baggini
AUGUSTINE   Henry Chadwick
BARTHES   Jonathan Culler
THE BIBLE   John Riches
BRITISH POLITICS
    Anthony Wright
BUDDHA   Michael Carrithers
BUDDHISM   Damien Keown
CAPITALISM   James Fulcher
THE CELTS   Barry Cunliffe
CHOICE THEORY
    Michael Allingham
CHRISTIAN ART   Beth Williamson
CLASSICS   Mary Beard and
    John Henderson
CLAUSEWITZ   Michael Howard
THE COLD WAR
    Robert McMahon

CONTINENTAL PHILOSOPHY
    Simon Critchley
COSMOLOGY   Peter Coles
CRYPTOGRAPHY
    Fred Piper and Sean Murphy
DADA AND SURREALISM
    David Hopkins
DARWIN   Jonathan Howard
DEMOCRACY   Bernard Crick
DESCARTES   Tom Sorell
DRUGS   Leslie Iversen
THE EARTH   Martin Redfern
EGYPTIAN MYTHOLOGY
    Geraldine Pinch
EIGHTEENTH-CENTURY
    BRITAIN   Paul Langford
THE ELEMENTS   Philip Ball
EMOTION   Dylan Evans
EMPIRE   Stephen Howe
ENGELS   Terrell Carver
ETHICS   Simon Blackburn
THE EUROPEAN UNION
    John Pinder
EVOLUTION
    Brian and Deborah Charlesworth
FASCISM   Kevin Passmore
THE FRENCH REVOLUTION
    William Doyle
FREUD   Anthony Storr
GALILEO   Stillman Drake
GANDHI   Bhikhu Parekh

Available soon:

AFRICAN HISTORY
  John Parker and Richard Rathbone
ANCIENT EGYPT Ian Shaw
THE BRAIN Michael O'Shea
BUDDHIST ETHICS
  Damien Keown
CHAOS Leonard Smith
CHRISTIANITY Linda Woodhead
CITIZENSHIP Richard Bellamy
CLASSICAL ARCHITECTURE
  Robert Tavernor
CLONING Arlene Judith Klotzko
CONTEMPORARY ART
  Julian Stallabrass
THE CRUSADES
  Christopher Tyerman
DERRIDA Simon Glendinning
DESIGN John Heskett
DINOSAURS David Norman
DREAMING J. Allan Hobson
ECONOMICS Partha Dasgupta
THE END OF THE WORLD
  Bill McGuire
EXISTENTIALISM Thomas Flynn
THE FIRST WORLD WAR
  Michael Howard
FREE WILL Thomas Pink
FUNDAMENTALISM
  Malise Ruthven
HABERMAS Gordon Finlayson

HIEROGLYPHS
  Penelope Wilson
HIROSHIMA B. R. Tomlinson
HUMAN EVOLUTION
  Bernard Wood
INTERNATIONAL RELATIONS
  Paul Wilkinson
JAZZ Brian Morton
MANDELA Tom Lodge
MEDICAL ETHICS
  Tony Hope
THE MIND Martin Davies
MYTH Robert Segal
NATIONALISM Steven Grosby
PERCEPTION Richard Gregory
PHILOSOPHY OF RELIGION
  Jack Copeland and Diane Proudfoot
PHOTOGRAPHY
  Steve Edwards
THE RAJ Denis Judd
THE RENAISSANCE
  Jerry Brotton
RENAISSANCE ART
  Geraldine Johnson
SARTRE Christina Howells
THE SPANISH CIVIL WAR
  Helen Graham
TRAGEDY Adrian Poole
THE TWENTIETH CENTURY
  Martin Conway

For more information visit our web site
www.oup.co.uk/vsi

Chris Gosden

PREHISTORY

A Very Short Introduction

OXFORD
UNIVERSITY PRESS

OXFORD
UNIVERSITY PRESS

Great Clarendon Street, Oxford OX2 6DP

Oxford University Press is a department of the University of Oxford.
It furthers the University's objective of excellence in research, scholarship,
and education by publishing worldwide in

Oxford New York

Auckland Bangkok Buenos Aires Cape Town Chennai
Dar es Salaam Delhi Hong Kong Istanbul Karachi Kolkata
Kuala Lumpur Madrid Melbourne Mexico City Mumbai Nairobi
São Paulo Shanghai Taipei Tokyo Toronto

Oxford is a registered trade mark of Oxford University Press
in the UK and in certain other countries

Published in the United States
by Oxford University Press Inc., New York

British Library Cataloguing in Publication Data

Data available

Library of Congress Cataloging in Publication Data

Data available

ISBN 978-0-19-280343-6

5 7 9 10 8 6

Typeset by RefineCatch Ltd, Bungay, Suffolk
Printed in Great Britain by
Ashford Colour Press, Gosport, Hants.

Contents

Acknowledgements

I would like to thank three people all called David, as chance would have it. My two friends David Morgan and David van Oss read this in manuscript form and gave me both stern criticism and encouragement, both equally important. My uncle, David Gosden, took me to the hillfort on Cold Kitchen Hill and to the excavations at South Cadbury when I was young and gave rise to my earliest interest in prehistory. Readers may have their own opinions as to whether he is to be thanked or blamed for this, but I am very grateful for it.

List of illustrations

The publisher and the author apologize for any errors or omissions in the above list. If contacted they will be pleased to rectify these at the earliest opportunity.

Prehistory and archaeology – a note

There is another book in this series by Paul Bahn called *Archaeology: A Very Short Introduction*. There is some potential for confusion about the difference between archaeology and prehistory. Archaeology usually designates the process of making sense of the past through finding, excavating, analysing, and dating the remains of human activity. Archaeology can be applied to any period of the past, even the most recent. Prehistory is the story we tell about the period before writing (although I use the term in slightly different manner here as you will see). In this book I shall not focus on how sites are found, dated, and analysed, but rather on the stories we tell of the past.

A very, very short introduction to chronology

The hard thing about writing a very short introduction to prehistory is that prehistory is so long. Human origins currently go back 6 million years, a time period which encompasses a number of different prehistoric and geological periods. Prehistory is about sets of sites, artefacts and landscapes from the past which we try to understand in the present, putting the evidence we have in the context of their contemporary environments, both physical and social. I will refer to commonly-used terms for periods of the past, and rather than pause to explain each of them in the text, provide some overview here. For each region of the world I have also constructed a series of very brief timelines at the back of the book.

Beneath me as I sit here in the centre of southern Britain lies the following general sequence of sediments and archaeological evidence. In the upper metre of soil and sub-soil is evidence from the last 10,000 years – what are locally known as the Mesolithic (*c.*8000–4000 BC – i.e. Before Christ) – a world of hunter-gatherers living in modern climatic conditions; the Neolithic period (*c.*4000–1800 BC) – the first farmers; the Bronze Age (1800–800 BC) – the first widespread use of metals; the Iron Age (800 BC–AD [Anno Domini] 43) – the end of prehistory. The period older than 10,000 years ago is known as the Palaeolithic and extends back to the start of direct human ancestry. The last 2 million years has been a period of fluctuating cold and warm periods known generally as the Ice Ages. Evidence from this period is found in river gravels, cave deposits and relatively rare occurrences of old sediments, as we shall see in the next chapter. The Palaeolithic currently starts 6 million years ago in Africa, where our earliest direct ancestors originated to spread out to Eurasia and southeast Asia between 1.8 and 1 million years ago (see Fig. 6 for a depiction of early hominid evolution). The oldest evidence in Britain is no older than this. At this stage of human evolution we are looking at *Homo erectus* – a stocky creature with a small brain, a limited social life and restricted material culture (although life may not have been as dull as this makes it sound). The so-called Ice Ages of the last 2 million years were really fluctuating climates and so in the Thames gravels beneath me are evidences of cold-adapted faunas (mammoths, woolly rhinos etc.) and warm-loving creatures, including hominids who may have lived in Europe only during warm periods. This was not true of the last glaciation, which started around 40,000 years ago and reached its height around 18,000 years ago. Now there were two sets of hominid species permanently in Europe – ourselves (*Homo sapiens sapiens*) and Neanderthals (*Homo neanderthalensis*) – the latter a cold-adapted species found from Britain to central Asia, whose extinction has led to one of the great whodunits – did we wipe them out directly, out-compete them more indirectly, or did they die out due to an inability to cope with changing conditions? At the height of the last glacial, the northern polar ice caps extended down to the Thames, with tundra south of that and open savannah conditions down to the Mediterranean. Much of Canada was covered by ice, and the expansion of the southern ice sheets caused glaciers in Tasmania, the Australian mainland and Argentina. Because so much of the earth's water had frozen and because ice is denser than water, global sea levels dropped, joining Britain to Europe, Papua New Guinea to Australia, and Borneo to peninsular Malaysia. There was drought in the tropical zones, extending the deserts and savannahs and creating holes in the equatorial rainforest. As the earth's climate warmed after 14,000 BC the ice retreated, and plants, animals, insects and birds moved into higher latitudes in both hemispheres and recolonized former deserts. Land was lost to the rising sea, especially in southeast Asia, and more continuous rainforest may have posed some barriers in the tropics. This cycle of warm and cold has been repeated a number of times over the last 2 million years.

Although a small part of the story in terms of overall time, we are most interested in people like us – *Homo sapiens sapiens*. We arose in Africa about 120,000 years ago, moving out to the Middle East by 90,000 years ago and the Indian sub-continent and beyond by 70,000. Europe and Australia were both colonized about 50,000 years ago, the latter for the first time, and the last large landmass to receive people was the Americas 20–15,000 years ago. After that the last big movements were to islands – the Caribbean and Mediterranean islands were permanently settled around 6000 BC, the remote Pacific islands after 1500 BC, with places like Iceland in the northern hemisphere and New Zealand in the southern being the last sizeable pieces of land people reached, about 1000 years ago.

The chronological scheme for understanding prehistory, the so-called Three Age system, was mainly developed in Europe. The Stone Age was divided into two by the start of farming, with the Old Stone Age (Palaeolithic, with its own three divisions – lower, middle and upper) succeeded by the New Stone Age (Neolithic). The metal ages of Bronze and Iron, it was thought, saw the development of tribal societies with sophisticated farming and the ability to build monuments like hillforts or create metal objects both for use and for long-distance exchanges. The Three Age system works fine for much of Eurasia (although not Japan) and with some reservations for southeast Asia. Australia and the Pacific had only stone ages; the first metals were introduced by Europeans. Africa's bronze age probably came after its iron age and the Americas developed only copper, eschewing bronze or iron. Reflecting their different histories the Americas have developed their own terminologies, sometimes aimed at understanding the growth of states and civilizations in central and southern America (Archaic, Formative,

Classic etc.) or local sequences in north America (Woodland, Anasazi etc.). Since the 1960s absolute dates, especially radiocarbon determinations, have come through in numbers providing the basis for a comparative world prehistory, so that we can now ask what was happening in the world 18,000 or 5000 BC. Absolute dates have not solved all our chronological problems, but have shifted attention from when things happened to why they happened.

Absolute dates have changed our views of processes. In many areas of the world we can now see that the adoption of farming, which used to be seen as a sudden and dramatic change, often happened over a long period of time. The acceptance of sheep, cattle, pigs, wheat, barley and oats over much of western Eurasia occurred slowly and through complicated means between 10,000 and 3000 BC in differing areas; the movement of rice, probably first domesticated in China around 6000 BC, to Japan, India and southeast Asia took many millennia, as did the movement of millet and sorghum in Africa or maize and beans in the Americas. Indeed, many now think that the origins of farming is not really the issue. More significant is the total, but changing, pattern of production and consumption, which includes not only plants and animals, but also stone tools, pots, baskets, textiles and metals. Over the last ten thousand years people have created a complex series of worlds for themselves drawing on even older skills and resources – but such issues take us beyond an introduction to chronology and I will leave them for later chapters.

Chapter 1
What and when is prehistory?

On the plain there lay a horse. Clustered tightly around it was a group of creatures intent on what they were doing; some watched the group of hyenas circling the dead animal, occasionally throwing stones to keep them off. Some still held their wooden spears.

Six had their heads down, working flint. They had already prepared some of the great nodules of local flint from the nearby sea cliff by taking off flakes to give the rough shape of a handaxe and now each was working a prepared chunk with great speed and skill. The other scavengers and predators kept away: they had tangled with these creatures before and learnt to keep a distance. As soon as the first knapper had finished the razor-sharp artefact that we now call a 'handaxe', they scrambled on to the horse carcass and began to cut the meat. Joints were taken from the legs and haunches and once the bones had been revealed the larger ones were smashed to extract the marrow. Let us imagine that the adults helped to feed the kids and the young aided the old, although the weaker members may have had to grab what they could. Some meat was consumed on the spot, the choicer joints were taken to the top of the cliff where the group had a base and consumed at leisure. Let us imagine again that they could relax now for a day or two, replace their

1. The Boxgrove hominids hunt a horse

spears, make a new hammer for flint working from a suitable horse bone, and play with their children.

This happened at a place which half a million years later would be known as Boxgrove, near Chichester in southern England. None of the creatures involved had the remotest awareness that traces of their activities would survive for half a million years, preserved by rapid burial under collapsing cliff sediments. No words survive to tell us of this and countless other incidents, but we can give voice to questions aplenty. Because Boxgrove is an extraordinary site there is a surprising number of things we can know with certainty. Beautifully detailed excavation and recording of the site has shown six (or perhaps seven) discrete areas of flint working where the handaxes were fashioned. Dealing with a three-dimensional jigsaw puzzle, archaeologists have worked in reverse order to the earlier hominids and, rather than breaking down a big nodule of flint into small flakes and a large handaxe, they have put the flakes back together again to create a complete nodule with only one missing

2

middle element – the handaxe itself. A void is left in the centre of the stone reminding us that in some parts of the world more recent stone knappers have seen their task as not making a stone tool, but rather freeing it from its encasing stone material. Once freed these particular handaxes have so far eluded archaeological detection, although they may lie in another part of the same site, discarded by a meat-bloated creature moving off to rest somewhere safe. Indeed many dozens of near-pristine handaxes have been recovered from Boxgrove, some with microscopic traces that indicate they were used for butchery.

The horse bones themselves tell their own story. This was the largest true horse species ever found in Britain, for a start, making a very attractive quarry for a hunting band. The horse bones that lie scattered amongst the flint debris show evidence of butchery in the form of thin scores into the surface of the bone resulting from the process of filleting to remove blocks of meat and muscle. The bones are smashed, probably with flint hammers, for marrow extraction. Microscopic examination shows the marks of animal teeth, with hyenas moving in after the hominids had left. We can tell which order various creatures got to the carcass as the teeth marks gouged across existing flint butchery marks, hyenas coming in to crunch the bone (and incidentally to scatter some of the flint debris a little in the process) after the hominids had left. In this set of coastal communities hyenas were not top dog and although working in a socially organized fashion themselves could not compete with the tools, intelligence, and organization of the hominids.

How do we know that these creatures had spears? Here we enter an area of slightly less certain inference. One scapula (shoulder blade) of the horse has a perfectly circular hole, which, on the basis of comparisons with holes made experimentally on modern skeletons, could probably only have been made by a pointed object travelling at a high velocity. This is not inconsistent with a spear thrown from a distance hitting the horse at considerable speed. Why use such equivocal language? The trivial reason is that the horse bone is somewhat chalky and flaky after its 500 millennia of burial, raising questions about the nature of the hole and how it got there, but really there is little doubt about the identification of the wound. The more important reason is that a lot hangs on whether these creatures hunted or not. Many have said that hunting only developed with fully modern humans some 50,000 years ago and in earlier times there was not the social cohesion, technology, or wit to do more than scavenge the kills of large carnivores or gather plant foods. To bring down, kill, and butcher a large fit horse is no easy task and makes us think about the nature of group organization, levels of physical skills, and mental acuity. It is not something most of us would like to do armed only by stone age technology.

Our humanity resides in social cooperation and a flexibility of mental and physical response to the world and we are fascinated by the origins of all these abilities. For creatures half a million years ago to appear to possess many of the things that make us human causes us to reflect on some of the deeper questions of human existence. These creatures were rather different to us in physical form, so what is the link between the nature of bodies and brains (biology, in short) and culture? Their range of material culture (at least that which survives) appears to lack elements of decoration and style we would associate with all modern material culture known from the last 50,000 years. Does this matter? Does it signal a less rounded and deep appreciation of the material and social worlds? Does the lack of apparent stylistic and symbolic content of their material culture indicate that these creatures lacked the most sophisticated symbolic system of all – language? Were gestures, grunts and the sharing of food all that passed between them? Or did they sit and discuss the killing of the horse for weeks and months afterwards? Of course we do not know and will never know for sure, but these are the questions that most interest us.

Archaeological excavation is often described as moving from the known to the unknown; working from deposits and sequences on areas of the site which are well understood to those which are not.

The process of inference that creates prehistory moves in a similar sequence. We start from the nature of knapping and butchery debris, which methods of reconstruction developed over the last century allow us to understand with some certainty. We then move from the reconstructed flint nodule with the ghost of a handaxe at its heart to the manual actions which produced it, the use of the missing tool for cutting up the horse, to the nature of social and physical skills lying behind these acts and on to their individual and social consequences. Prehistorians need to exercise extreme vigilance, both for themselves and for others, as to when they cross the line between being reasonably sure about something into less directly grounded inference. The issues we are driven to understand lie always in the areas of least uncertainty, so that too cautious an approach will leave us grounded in the fascinating but ultimately trivial world of stone tool technologies or butchery practices. We can throw caution to the winds, especially in a synthetic volume such as this, pursuing the big picture, straying increasingly far from the secure inferences that stone or bone analysts can provide, exciting their rightful scorn – 'There is no way you can be sure of *that*.'

Writing prehistory is a question of balance. The immense scope of prehistory (some 6 million years or so at present) poses the big questions of what makes us human both as individuals and members of groups. The difficulty and paucity of our evidence leaves us uncomfortably aware that the imaginative effort needed to understand the past can easily lead to fantasy, to projecting our common-sense views of the world onto the big screen of human prehistory. Writing a prehistory partly derives from the results of archaeology, from the things that people have dug up and made sense of, and partly from critical awareness of our biases and taken-for-granteds. A central paradox of prehistory is that we are interested in the past because it was different from the present, so that the study of prehistory can add vital new insights into humanity past and present. But because prehistory was different, it cannot be understood as we understand the world today.

If a time machine were to take us back to the Boxgrove beach flats half a million years ago we would be profoundly shocked by what we found. The hominid group would not act in ways that we could immediately understand (they would not act like other apes or like fully modern humans) and we would probably be less interested in studying them than surviving. Would they let us join the group or see us a threat and how would we find out without fatal consequences? Would there be mutual recognition of some shared humanity separating us from other species? Or would they feel more related to the hyenas, a constant, intimate part of their lives, than to us? If we joined the group could we develop any useful skills to benefit it? I'm not sure I could learn to bring a running horse down with a yew spear or make a good handaxe and cut meat before the hyenas moved in, but I might have been able to look after the kids. What would the grit in the horse meat do to our fillings? What would our responsibility be towards the group? Should we tell them that the most severe glacial cold ever experienced in Britain would drive their descendants from the area? Or suggest that cooked food might be a good idea? Coming back to the present our detailed field notes and video footage would be leapt on by media and academia alike, but would a snapshot of life half a million years ago be necessarily more informative than the fragmentary, but long-term, history provided by archaeology? All these are questions without easy and obvious answers.

Boxgrove takes us back to an early stage in European prehistory. For a while, it had a good claim to be the earliest site in Britain (there are now sites which might be twice that old). *The Times* described a tibia from the site as evidence of the 'first European'. Certainly it is still by far the best preserved and most skilfully excavated site from such an early period. Obviously no spoken or written records survive from this period (in the absence of our hypothetical time-travellers) and this is the definition of prehistory. It is the time before words. Prehistory is the sense we make of our physical evidence. What form should prehistory take, if we cannot write the sorts of detailed accounts of the past that are possible once we have written or oral histories? Does the length and breadth of prehistoric evidence compensate for its human depth, our lack of access to everyday experience, thought, and feeling? These are central questions which I shall try to throw some light on in the course of what follows.

Ending prehistory

We have started to look at what prehistory might be, but have not tackled the question of when it was. Boxgrove provides a window into the deep past of Britain. As chance would have it, prehistory ended when Julius Caesar landed on the south coast not that many miles away from Boxgrove. The authors of *1066 and All That* began their memorable history of Britain (composed of only those dates and events that most people remember) 'The first date in English history is 55 BC in which year Julius Caesar (the *memorable* Roman Emperor) landed, like all other successful invaders of these islands, at Thanet.' The fact that Caesar was not an emperor should not detract from the overall truth of the statement, that British history starts, although patchily, with Caesar's accounts of his invasion. This proto-historical period only gained more thorough historical coverage later in the Roman period and even then there are many areas of life unilluminated by written accounts. Although late in comparison to places like Mesopotamia which have histories some 3,000 years before Caesar, the passage from prehistory to history long predates that found in many parts of the world. In some places, like Papua New Guinea, prehistory has ended within the living memory of the oldest people.

Ongka was terrified. I shall let him use his own words (in translation) to describe the events. The fact that his words survive is crucial.

> When the first planes of the white men came, I was down by a stream. There were several of us, old men and young boys, all working at shaping stone axes. I thought I heard one of the

marsupials that growl as they go along and have tails like lizards' tails. We chased the noise through the undergrowth; it kept moving in front of us and we couldn't catch it. Then we looked up and saw it was in the sky and we said 'It's a kind of witchcraft come to strike us and eat us up!' We argued about it: was it really witchcraft, or was it a big hornbill or an eagle? Some said it was a thunderclap gone mad and come down from the sky. Then it went away and we said that we would find out about it later. . . . Later we saw Jim Taylor himself, [Taylor was a government officer accompanying Mick and Dan Leahy, two gold prospectors, into the New Guinea Highlands] he came through and called out for supplies for his many carriers. People took sugar-cane, sweet potatoes, bananas and pigs to him. He would draw out of his long trouser pockets a big mottled cowrie shell of the kind we valued, and show it to them and they said 'Oh! He has a big cowrie and he's drawn it out of his own behind!' That was how we got to know the white man. (Ongka 1979: 5–6)

Prehistory ended for Ongka and others of the Kawelka group at 10 a.m. on 8 March 1933 when the Leahy's expedition first flew over the New Guinea Highlands in a chartered Junkers biplane looking for promising areas for gold prospecting.

Two weeks later they walked in, the first white people to enter the densely populated New Guinea Highlands, bringing an end to prehistory in the process. The axe-making expedition that Ongka was on was probably the last ever carried out by the Kawelka, as stone was replaced by steel as a chopping tool and by the now common seashells as a form of brideprice. The end of prehistory was filmed by Mick Leahy, who took a 16 mm movie camera with him, making several hours of film, as well as taking over 5,000 35 mm still photographs with a Leica, and these have subsequently been incorporated into a film called *First Contact* by Anderson and Connolly, together with the testimony of local people who remember these events.

Most prehistories do not end quite as suddenly as that of the New

2. Ongka in discussion

Guinea Highlands. The groups of interior New Guinea were some of the last in the world to enter the ambit of historical documentation, a process which first started 5,000 years ago. The earliest writing that we know of comes from the Eanna Temple complex at Uruk, a site in Mesopotamia (in present-day Iraq). Writing comes in the form of *bullae*, hollow clay balls with seal impressions all over their surface, which often contain a number of little clay tokens. The impressions, which are soon transferred to flat clay tablets, are pretty variable but recognizably ancestral to cuneiform signs, which first arise roughly 3000 BC. The earliest impressions are pictographic in form – little pictures that are stylized versions of the things they represent. And most of the things they represent are plants and animals. The earliest writing derived from vision rather than sound. Syllabic scripts, which were phonetically based, only appeared gradually and were able to represent both abstract concepts, for which there could be no picture, and the sound of the language. It was only when Akkadian took over from Sumerian as the main spoken language after 2300 BC that syllabic text really came into its own. The first scripts were not used for poetry or forms of creative expression, but for accountancy: keeping a track of plants, animals, and craft products from the point of production through various forms of exchange. Here is one immediate attraction of prehistory – it is the period before accountants came to dominate the earth. Only later was epic poetry recorded in script, with *The Epic of Gilgamesh* having a claim to being the first written poem that survives. Elsewhere writing was developed at much the same time, but probably under Mesopotamian influence. The hieroglyphic scripts of Egypt are totally different in form to cuneiform, but there is evidence of influence from Mesopotamia and a lack of indications of any precursors to writing such as are found in the Mesopotamian *bullae*. The Elamite scripts of Iran took inspiration from cuneiform and both scripts probably influenced the early writing systems of the Indus (present-day Pakistan and India). China clearly had its own trajectory towards writing, but also using a pictographic script, as did groups in central America, such as the Aztecs and the Mayas.

The start of history is not a single event or process, with records starting gradually and for a variety of reasons.

Prehistory ends gradually for a number of reasons. The drive to account for things excluded most of life from consideration, so that there is little real historical documentation of many aspects of most people's lives. The domestic arrangements, the nature of childhood, the relationships between women and men or between people and their gods, the daily round of work and leisure, can only be reconstructed for later periods and used to throw light on the earlier ones. The lack of abstract concepts in the early pictographic scripts means that our desires to understand abstract philosophies or forms of love and hate go unrequited for the first millennium that scripts existed. In many areas periods where writing is found are interspersed with 'dark ages' without literacy. The pictographic script of the Minoans which developed from around 1600 BC onwards was first deciphered by Michael Ventris using code-breaking techniques developed in the Second World War. The script was pictographic, but could also be shown to be an early form of Greek, which was a surprise to many as it indicated long-term continuities between at least the late Bronze Age and the present. Like the Mesopotamians the Minoans at palaces like Knossos were obsessive list makers, recording the trivia of production and transactions in a manner that makes both fascinating and eye-glazing reading. We learn a lot about sheep rearing, textile production, and pots and pans, but almost nothing about the textures of people's lives.

Then about 1200 BC the line goes dead. The palaces collapse in both Crete and mainland Greece, taking with them a need for a script. We re-enter a period of prehistory.

From the eighth century BC writing reappears, but this time it is the Greek syllabic script (taken from the Phoenicians) which lasts, albeit in an evolving form, down to the present. Unlike the previous Linear B script of the accountants we now hear the voice of a poet.

3. The Linear B script and its translation

'Two tripod-cauldrons of Cretan workmanship, of ai-ke-u type; one tripod-cauldron with a (?) single handle (?) on one foot; one tripod-cauldron of Cretan workmanship burnt away at the legs, (?) unserviceable; three (?) wine-jars; one larger-sized dipas with four handles; two larger-sized dipas with three handles; one smaller-sized dipas with four handles; one smaller-sized dipas with three handles; one smaller-sized dipas without handle.'

There is much debate about the person and writings of the poet Homer (was he one person or a set of traditions personified in a single name; how far do his tales reflect the world-view of the previous Bronze Age society or views more contemporary with when they were written down?). What we can be sure of is that story of the Trojan War has stayed with us until the present, to be joined by the later philosophy of Socrates, Plato and Aristotle as part of the foundations of Western culture. Although ancient historical traditions have been reinvented and remade through the Roman world, the Renaissance and the Enlightenment and although much of the influence of Aristotle on Europe came through the Arabic world, there is a continuity of written tradition between eighth-century Greece and the present that is not found with earlier periods, whose scripts needed to be discovered anew and deciphered. Issues of continuity and discontinuity of written traditions make us realize that not all forms of writing are the same, so that not all historical periods produce histories of the same type. For much of written history, the ability to read and write has been restricted to the elite and gives us a record (partial at that) of their interests and views of the world. Of the mass of humanity we learn little or nothing.

There are also penumbras around history, sometimes known as proto-history. Such forms would include Julius Caesar's account of southern Britain during his abortive invasion of 55 and 54 BC. *Veni, vidi, vici* is a compelling rhetorical statement by a master of the art, but without much information content or historical accuracy. We cannot take the accounts of the (would-be) victors at face value. More intriguing is the account of a journey, probably to Britain via Gaul, by Pytheas the Greek in the third century BC, an account which does not survive today but can be painstakingly reconstructed from secondary sources. And what are we to make of the Incas who used a system of knotted strings tied to a circular string (the *quipu*), but lacked any written script? The use of the *quipu* disappeared soon after the Spanish invasion and we don't really know how it worked. The knots on the strings probably acted as mnemonics for a system of knowledge mainly held in specialists' heads, with the positions of knots on various strings reminding the specialists of knowledge they had painfully committed to memory. Once the specialists had disappeared, due to the destructive effects of the Spanish invasion, the knots lost their meaning. The Incas are a rare, possibly unique, case of state organization that survived without a script and a method of accounting, putting them halfway between history and prehistory as these terms are generally defined.

If prehistory is such a hazy concept, why do we bother with it and what use does it serve? The word was first used in 1832, but only really came into common use after the publication of Sir John Lubbock's *Prehistoric Times* in 1865 (still in print in 1912, a true Victorian best-seller). Alternative terms, such as ante-history, never took off. The concept became really necessary because of an expansion of the imaginative universe during the 19th century and the opening up of larger expanses of time for biological and human history. At the beginning of that century most people who thought about it at all believed in a biblical chronology, taking the book of Genesis literally. Bishop Ussher at the end of the 18th century estimated that the earth was created in 4004 BC, which seems to us ludicrous not just in its brevity, but also its precision. Such an estimate might seem a mildly amusing by-product of an older intellectual history (although we are all aware that our own mistakes will occasion a wry smile a century from now) if it were not for the fact that belief in a short history for the earth is again growing. Creationist belief centres around the factual accuracy of the Bible as a guide to world history and the crucial role of God, as divine creator, in that history. The debate between archaeologists and creationists is seen as part of an ongoing argument between science and religion, with the creationists decrying an arid science that undermines sustaining forms of faith and belief and the archaeologists asserting the importance of concepts and results that are open to questioning, criticism, and re-evaluation. Prehistory represents a battle-ground for different world-views: the archaeologists envisaging some 6 million years back to the time of our earliest human ancestor, creationists denying the existence of any prehistory as the whole of our existence is covered from Genesis onwards.

Prehistory suffers from implicit links with illiteracy. To be civilized is to be literate, so that reading and writing are the basis of all education and much of our cultivation as cultured and sensitive human beings. People lacking the ability to read and write are cut off from many worlds of imagination, education, and experience. Not only are prehistoric periods those from which our evidence is deficient, but they are also periods when people's lives were deficient as they lacked the civilizing influences of written words. Such views are implicit in our attitudes to the past, rather than explicitly voiced prejudices, but they have their effects just the same. There are opposing views of course, held by people with different cultural values. For Aboriginal people in Australia, the concept of prehistory is suspect. The whole of human and pre-human history is contained in the notion of the Dreaming. The Dreaming was a period of time, infinitely far back in the past, when ancestors moved across the landscape creating the shape of that landscape and giving it cosmological significance. A stand of trees, a rock formation, or a river were all created by snakes, sharks, goannas, or other ancestral forms and given not just a shape, but a role in people's lives, so that some places were dangerous, some had beneficial powers and some ambiguous. People in the present have a duty to protect the landscape and to treat it in the right way and such duties are recorded and encoded in stories, dance, and forms of art. Initiation into society is through an education in these forms of knowledge, the most powerful of which is restricted to a few. Prior to the coming of whites in 1788 nothing was written down, but all significant history was recorded and transmitted in culturally appropriate forms. The concept of prehistory, telling of a forgotten time beyond the reach of written histories that needs to be discovered through archaeology, is puzzling and potentially offensive, making for difficult relationships between Aboriginal people and non-Aboriginal archaeologists. In such situations prehistory is an arena of debate and knowledge about the past that is intimately involved with control of life in the present.

Prehistory is mute and silent. It is history with all the words taken out. To many this seems not to leave a lot and they yearn for some direct evidence of the thoughts, feelings, and experiences of people from the prehistoric past. Not only is it wasteful to hope for things that cannot exist, but, much more importantly, this misses the point of what prehistory can tell us. Words are only a part of human experience. Me the writer and you the reader of this book are pretty logocentric; we like words, their sounds and meanings, and especially their written form. All our schooling and much of our experience have put words at the centre of our lives. But there is more to life than that. Many of our physical skills, our abilities to sense and appreciate material things and other people, do not derive from words nor can what pleases, disturbs, or bores us about the world easily be put into words. It is our experience of the physical and social world outside words that links us with prehistory and it is the nature of this experience I want to explore.

Prehistory puzzles 1

Before moving on, let us think about *your* prehistory. Prehistory is the aspect of life that lies beyond the reach of words. Most of prehistory is in the past, but all of our lives have elements which we find difficult to put into words, mainly because they are the bits of our lives we take for granted. Familiar objects and the skills to use them are basic aspects of everyone's existence. Familiarity can breed contempt, but also can give basic emotional and practical shape to everyday life. I once ran a class on material culture studies in a university in Melbourne, where I used to teach. As an ice-breaker and to get people to think about material things on a personal level I asked the class to fill an imaginary cubic metre of space with things that both told the story of their lives and which meant much to them. Two students' reactions stick in my mind. One said that he had already done this in reality. His house on the edge of Melbourne had been threatened by the Ash Wednesday bushfires in 1983, so that he and his family had been told to evacuate their house taking only a carload of things for the four of them. They had to make an almost instantaneous choice and went for things that told the story of their individual lives and their history as a family – a violin, a painting kit, jewellery, favourite toys for the kids, and the family photo album, plus a change of clothes each. He said they all realized without giving it much thought that without certain objects their lives would never be the same again and these were the ones they took. Fortunately their house did not burn down, but their feeling about the house and the things in it had changed irrevocably. The second student talked not long after her father died and had been buried. She said that the most affecting part of the service was when each member of the immediate family placed an object in the grave which most reminded them of their father and their relationship with him. The grave was filled in and the objects were buried with him. She said that picking the objects had made them all think deeply about their father, their relationship, and their loss, and helped them grieve an unexpected death.

What happens if you perform the same thought experiment? What areas of life are crucial, derive mainly from an attachment to objects, and lie partly beyond the scope of words? With what would you fill your cubic metre of space or sum up a relationship to someone very close? We all have our prehistories, even in this best documented of all centuries, and they are vital to our emotional, intellectual, and social well-being.

Chapter 2
The problems of prehistory

The idea of prehistory arose gradually between the 16th and early 19th centuries, but grew large and influential through debates about evolution in the middle of the 19th century. The establishment of a long prehistory is one of the great achievements of that century, as important in its own way in changing peoples' views of the world as the voyages of discovery of the previous 300 years. The discovery of the Americas was a profound shock to Europeans, leading them to question where all the peoples of the Americas came from, as none were mentioned in the Bible, and what sorts of relationships created and spread various peoples around the world. The discovery of a long prehistory had the same impact as finding a new continent, with its own myriad and strange ways of life, except that some of the inhabitants of the continent of prehistory were definitely ancestral to those writing prehistory. For places like Britain where identity is and was an issue, ancestry was problematical – should Britons derive their ancestry from the Normans, the Anglo-Saxons, the Romans, or now the Celts and indeed possibly pre-Celtic peoples? If Britons are people of mixed ancestry, how does one evaluate the mix of language, genes, artefacts, and landscapes that derives from the past? The same questions arise for Nigerians, Brazilians, Americans, or Chinese.

National and personal identities were problematical, and also those of race and class as we shall see, but there were deeper issues of identity that came to the surface through 19th-century debates which have never gone away. In a legendary meeting of the British Association for the Advancement of Science in the University Museum of Natural History in Oxford, Saturday 30 June 1860, the bishop of Oxford, 'Soapy Sam' Wilberforce, confronted Thomas Huxley, 'Darwin's Bulldog', in front of an audience of some 700 people. It was a meeting of high emotion where Lady Baxter fainted, the audience gasped, laughed, and applauded and no holds were barred (at least in the legendary accounts that are best remembered now). 'Soapy Sam' did ask Huxley whether he was descended from a monkey on his grandmother's or his grandfather's side, but the reply that it was better to be descended from a monkey than a bishop, came not from Huxley but from Hooker, another pro-Darwinite.

This half-remembered confrontation crystallized the spirit of the debate, which appeared to be about the remote past, but in fact concerned people's personal identity in the present. Darwin had long delayed the publication of *The Origin of Species*, which appeared in 1859, afraid of the controversy it would cause and the possible damage to his standing as a member of the establishment. A more complicated reception awaited his work than he anticipated, which was seized upon by different strands of thought and belief, as a perfect test of where people stood on issues of history and empiricism versus faith. Part of the origin myth of prehistory for us is that the acceptance of a long prehistory meant a rejection of a biblical chronology which put the origin of the world at 4004 BC, and was thus part of a victory of reason over superstition, science over religion. Here lies the continuing interest of the 1860 debate which looks like a cameo version of a broader clash of social values. However, the scientists often came from a particular set of religious backgrounds, such as Quakerism, which always placed emphasis on empirical investigation and personally derived truths, in contrast to more established religious forms amongst which the Bible was the crucial truth. All controversies in the 19th century were to some extent religious controversies, due to the greater religiosity of the age. It was only in the 20th century and a more secular society that science confronted religion in a more simplistic fashion. Evolution and prehistory are now real shibboleths for extreme views on both sides, with the nature of children's education a crucial litmus test. Prehistorians are seen to be on the side of the apes, rather than the angels, and are generally proud of the fact.

The excavation of Brixham Cave in 1858 was a crucial step towards the scientific acceptance of high human antiquity. Classical Darwinian theory, centred around the idea of descent with modification, held that the modifications from generation to generation made offspring either better suited to their contemporary environmental conditions, less suited, or made no difference at all. Those better suited had an increased chance of surviving to produce their own offspring, passing on their beneficial characteristics; those less suited were more likely to die before having offspring: hence the survival of the fittest, a biological encoding of the competitive spirit of capitalism. For Darwin change proceeded through small modifying steps and needed long periods of time to work itself out, especially once one thought of all the changes needed to move from single-celled organisms to the full complexity of human beings. It was impossible to see how this might be fitted into the biblical chronology of only 6,000 years since the creation of the earth. Empirical support for longer timescales poured in from geologists and biologists. For the first half of the 19th century there had been debate about the 'antiquity of man', to use the then contemporary terminology, surrounding a number of sites which might produce firm evidence that human beings had existed in the company of extinct animals, such as mammoths and woolly rhino, not mentioned in the Bible. For Victorians, seeing was believing and the site of Brixham provided visual proof of human antiquity. On 29 July 1858, Pengelly, a founder member of the Torquay Natural History Society and organizer of the excavations of the fissure known as the Bone Cave at Brixham, found his first flint tool from beneath 3 inches of stalagmite and in association with the

BRIXHAM.

GREAT NATURAL CURIOSITY.

INTERESTING EXHIBITION ! !

THE

"Ossiferous Cavern"

Recently discovered on Windmill Rea Common, will be exhibited for a short time only, by Mr. PHILP, who has just disposed of it to a well-known scientific gentleman.

Those who delight in contemplating the mysterious and wonderful operations of nature, will not find their time, or money mis-spent, in exploring this remarkable Cavern, and as the fossils are about to be removed, persons desirous of seeing them had better apply early.

Many gentlemen of acknowledged scientific reputation, have affirmed that the stalactitic formations are of the most unique and interesting character, presenting the most fantastic and beautiful forms of crystallization, representing every variety of animal and vegetable structure.

Here too, may be seen the relics of animals that once roamed over the Earth before the post-tertiary period, or human epoch.

THE BONES AND TEETH, &c., OF

HYENAS, TIGERS, BEARS,

LARGE FOSSIL HORNS

of a Stag, all grouped and arranged by an eminent Geologist.

N.B. Strangers may obtain particulars of the locality, &c., of the Cavern, on application to Mr. BROWN, of the Bolton Hotel; or at the residence of the Proprietor, Spring Gardens.

THE CHARGE FOR ADMISSION TO THE "CAVERN," SIXPENCE.
Children will be admitted for FOURPENCE.

ated. Brixham. June 10th. 1858.

EDWARD FOX, PRINTER, &c., BRIXHAM.

4. The initial announcement of finds from Brixham Cave, where later stone tools were found in association with extinct animals

bones of rhinos and hyenas. Visits were made by the gentlemen scholars of the various geological, archaeological, and anthropological societies, who were impressed by the care and precision of Pengelly's excavation and recording, but most struck by the association between undoubted human products and extinct animals coming from a different and earlier phase in the earth's history. Rapid reassessment occurred of other sites, not least those of the Somme gravels (where the later battle was fought), previously disparaged by the British as French hyperbole, where stone tools had also been found with rhino bones some metres below the surface.

Having visited Brixham and Abbéville in northern France, Sir Charles Lyell, Britain's most influential geologist, put aside his earlier scepticism about the 'age of man' and addressed the British Association of the Advancement of Science meeting in Aberdeen on 18 September 1859. For Lyell to change his mind was a sign that the British intellectual establishment was opening up to the possibility that prehistory was immensely long, placing recent ways of life in stark perspective. In his talk Lyell mentioned in passing the forthcoming publication of a book which, he felt, would have some influence on thinking about issues of timescale and the relationships between people and nature – this was *The Origin of Species*, to appear on 24 November 1859.

One outcome of Darwinian thought is modern genetics. The Human Genome Project, which seeks to sequence the whole of a single human genome for the first time, has concluded that we each have some 30,000 genes, about a third the number in previous estimates. In many ways the smallness of our genome is a conclusive demonstration of ideas stemming from Darwin, which emphasize that we are part of nature, as we share the majority of our genes with other species. A letter writer to the *Guardian* newspaper said that he no longer knows whether he is a man or a mouse, as there is surprisingly little genetic difference between the two. On the other hand, our genetic closeness to all other species underlines the fact that we are different. Our shared genetic inheritance makes it pretty well impossible to argue for a genetic basis for culture. There are not enough genes only found in humans to find a basis for cultural complexity there. People are cultural, I would argue, not due to biology but because we have involved material things so deeply in our social relations (see Chapter 3). Some see a culture–nature divide, where human life is all about creating domesticated landscapes, plants, animals, and artefacts, the human imprint on which is so overwhelming that we have to assign these to culture and not nature. Nature is 'red in tooth and claw' and is the part of the world that has escaped human influence. Some of nature is not outside us, but within, giving us an instinctive basis for life, usually seen in terms of the selfishness of the individual (or their genes) locked in a struggle with all other organisms (human or not) in order to thrive. But not everyone in the world divides nature and culture.

All understandings of the world are both socially based and constructed through action in the world which teaches us about the properties of the world. All humans carry around preconceptions of the ways in which the world works, which are put at risk through action. It goes without saying that we all see the world in our own image, but we can be proved wrong. A stress on the individual as the unit of selection and as the basis for the struggle of each against each makes good sense to Westerners, who have had 200 years of social and cultural encouragement to see themselves as sovereign individuals. Not everyone sees the world in the same way.

For instance, the Mbuti Pygmies of the Ituri rainforest in Zaire refer to the forest as either 'Mother' or 'Father' and this is not just because it gives them food, warmth, clothing, and shelter. Just like a parent, the forest gives them affection. The Batek Negritos of Malaysia see themselves as having an intimate set of relationships with the plants, animals, and *hala'* (the creator spirits who made both people and the forest world and exercise care over it). In understanding such feelings about the world, Tim Ingold has argued, we should not see the primary relations as being social ones (parent–child) which are then projected onto the natural world (the forest), but to see that all these conceptions and relations are one and the same. Society does not exist before nature or vice versa, but both exist within a seamless network of relationships that unfold through action. Forests have intentions and emotions too, to which human beings have to pay attention, so that hunting and gathering in the forest is not just a matter of right technology or training, but of respect and an understanding for all the relationships people are enmeshed within. To create an evolutionary biology along these lines (if it were culturally necessary or possible) would not start from the selfish gene or the individual, as concepts such as selfishness or the individual would not come easily to the Mbuti, for instance.

If we are trying to understand hunter-gatherers in Europe 20,000 years ago can we assume that they had similar feelings and world-views to hunter-gatherers today? The answer to this question is obviously 'no'. We can't make such an assumption. Equally obviously we cannot assume that our approach to the world, our own cosmology, will be appropriate, although many start their analysis on this basis. A cosmology lays out expectations about how relationships will unfold, whether these are between people or with other elements of the world. A cosmology also specifies how relationships ought to work, whether through respect, antagonism, care, or avoidance. Cosmologies have both a physical and a metaphysical element, describing how the world works, how it should work in a moral sense and the responsibilities that entails. Our sciences, such as biology, have a cosmological basis, deriving from more generally held social and cultural values, and this is also true of other peoples' ways of life. Imaginative understanding is needed to appreciate the cosmologies of others and we need to beware of the fine line that separates our imagination from fantasy, a constant problem in understanding prehistory.

We need some mental tools to understand the lives of others, especially when we are working from artefacts, sites, and landscapes without the benefit of words. A key term is relationship. What we might take to be entities, such as people or objects, exist not in and through themselves, but through their relationships with others. We are all aware that in different situations we become slightly different people. With our parents we act differently than with our children and with one friend we may talk sport and politics and with another explore our psychological states or family relationships. The meeting of groups of friends can be uncomfortable as they each expect from you a particular sort of relationship and personality. If we take the principle that relationships alter people and write it larger, we can see that various social forms value and privilege certain sorts of relationships over others, and a single person may move through networks of relations changing as they go. A society is made up of a particular spectrum of relationships, not found elsewhere, and people move through parts of this spectrum as they move through life. We should not expect men always to exhibit attributes of males (locally defined), but to develop female characteristics under some circumstances, and women can explore maleness. Gender attributes are never entirely fixed or invariant and nor is any other aspect of people's identity. This includes the degree to which people exist as separable individuals or as parts of a group. As again we are aware, sometimes we stand out as individuals, when we have to make a presentation, are brought before a court, or have a party thrown in our honour. On such occasions our own personal actions are apparent and our responsibility for these might be under question. At other times, such as watching a good film or at the family exchange of Christmas presents, we exist primarily as part of a group, sharing emotions with others and having these emotions reinforced because they are shared.

As we have seen, relationships do not just exist between people but between people and things. Imagine the wearer of the Sunghir necklace made of 3,000 beads who lived 18,000 years ago (see

Chap. 3), standing on the snow in what is now northern Russia. She would have been clothed in furs, neatly sown and possibly decorated, she probably had eye goggles to cut the glare, snowshoes to walk around on, and possibly sleds and other contrivances. Stone, bone, and antler tools existed in abundance on a settlement where there were houses made of mammoth bone. Two children were buried within the settlement at Sunghir with ivory beads sown into their caps and clothing, as well as having figurines and ivory spears. In a marginal environment in the last Ice Age up by the Arctic Circle, people had created a rich world for themselves, where their social position and links to others were created in and through complicated forms of material culture. Let us think also of the Highlands of New Guinea 6,000 years before Ongka lived there, where tropical heat is only modified by altitude and which became the site of an independent invention of agriculture. High up in the central mountain cordillera people learnt to drain swamps in order to plant large root crops, such as taro, and tree crops like bananas. Those with access to swamp land that they had learnt to use productively were better able to engage in exchanges of axes, shells, and bird of paradise plumes, exchanges all ultimately underwritten by the production of food. People created and defined themselves socially through the objects they made and used, exploring new dimensions to humanity. It is the variety of human dimensions that is ultimately interesting to us; prehistory is when so many dimensions were explored and expanded.

Part of learning about the past is an unlearning of the present, questioning and perhaps jettisoning values that we hold dear. Understanding prehistory is both an empirical and a philosophical business. We need excavations and surveys to provide secure information about the past; equally we must question how we live, think, and feel in order to open our imaginations to other orders of life which make different sense of the same world.

To a great extent, prehistory has investigated the origins of people like 'Us'. In its 19th-century origins prehistory was created mainly by the white, male middle classes who appeared secure in their identity and superiority. The heat generated by early debates over evolution and human antiquity show that the participants were anything but secure, in a period where religion confronted science, international imperial links reconfigured issues of class and the role of the nation state, and notions such as the 'primitive' were used to create as much distance as possible from the working classes and the colonial masses. Darwin is a good leitmotif for the times, his constant ill health a physical expression of his worry about the human implications of evolution and its reception by his peers. Prehistory was born as a series of steps and stages taking humanity from people like Them – unfortunate hunter-gatherers living at the mercy of a fickle environment, i.e. savages – to people like Us – those enjoying an urbane lifestyle made possible through the progressive application of the powers of reason which have given people control over the physical world through the invention of farming (barbarism), cities (civilization), and industrialism/ imperialism.

Even for Europeans the triumphalist story of prehistory has always been counter-posed by a darker tale – Marx decrying the fact that the material wealth of capitalism had been bought at the expense of spiritual impoverishment; Weber mourning the loss of magic in a specialized, routinized, and bureaucratic world; Freud analysing civilization and its discontents; Woody Allen, most succinctly, saying that 'My one regret in life is that I am not somebody else'. Prehistory stretches narrative strands between the twin poles of then and now, and the tension holding those strands taut depends upon our conception of those twin poles. Prehistory as it still exists today was born in a revolutionary moment in the middle of the 19th century when there was rapid reassessment of past and present, so that tension was palpable. By the end of the 19th century the shock of our animal nature had been buried under a story of the emancipation from our original state through the application of reason, materialized as technology. By the end of the 20th century

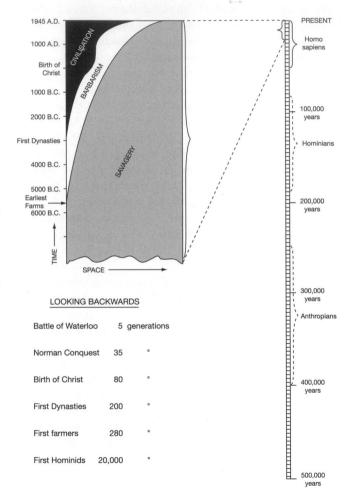

5. Prehistory as a movement from savagery through barbarism to civilization

the reasonableness of civilization was harder to accept. The movement out of empire had made Western superiority seem a dubious basis from which to write history, and the exploration of elements of the human personality other than the faculty for reason was gathering pace. Tension has re-entered the writing of prehistory. Quite what the relationship between past and present is right now varies throughout the world depending on the intellectual and political climate, a variation that I shall explore in what follows.

Prehistory puzzles 2

Archaeology has been described as the science of rubbish. Prehistory is the sense we make of that rubbish. In the early 1970s a group of archaeologists set up the so-called Tucson Garbage Project, under the leadership of Bill Rathje, working in the city of that name in southern Arizona. Their aim was to find out how what people threw away reflected the way that they lived and their patterns of consumption. Tucson then had some 360,000 inhabitants, over a quarter of whom were of Mexican descent. The city's 66 urban census districts were sampled to get a range of areas with different ethnic backgrounds, economic status, and age.

Garbage was analysed from 19 census districts by the Tucson Sanitation Division and over 300 student volunteers (having had suitable injections) sorted the rubbish into different categories of food and household waste. For three census districts, interviews were carried out to match people's accounts of their consumption with what went into the bin. There were considerable differences between 'front door' and 'back door' evidence. Some were unsurprising. Beer consumption was generally underestimated, although middle class households were more accurate than working class ones. Of the 33 households who said they never bought beer only 12 discarded no beer cans. One 'non-consuming' household threw away enough cans to make up three and a half cases. Part of the reason for the mismatch was that many of the poor households lived on government food stamps, which couldn't be used to buy beer, and didn't want their beer-buying habits to come to official attention.

Poorer households consumed less economically than richer ones. Unable to buy detergent or cereal in large cheap packs because money was short, they bought what they could, when they could. Households with larger and more predictable incomes were able to make economies of scale in their purchases. There was a beef shortage in 1973 during which the amount of beef thrown away increased. The researchers felt that this was because people bought beef in large amounts when it was available and then, unable to eat it all, threw more than normal away. Rathje and his team estimated that during 1974 some 9,500 tons of once-edible food ended up in landfills, food worth $9–$11 million at 1974 prices. Rathje subsequently went on to do an archaeology of landfill sites, coring down through strata of rubbish to help complete his understanding of the waste disposal cycle.

How far do you think what goes into your bin reflects your age, income, and class? How accurately are you able to estimate what you consume and what you discard? Do any of us really know what happens to the rubbish we generate once it leaves our dustbins? What sorts of new political and personal policies are needed to deal with the mountains of rubbish we generate?

The Tucson Garbage Project helped illustrate further the gap between words and our relationships with things, some of the gaps predictable. We talk and think about consumption in one way, but the rubbish we generate provides a different story. In periods without written records, this rubbish is the whole story; where words are preserved they demonstrate the tension between conscious thought and speech, and action.

Chapter 3
Human skills
and experiences

The changing haircuts, the extravagant lifestyle, the obsession with
fashion might make it difficult for many to accept or appreciate the
nature of Beckham's intelligence (do substitute the sportsperson of
your choice, if Beckham or football are unfamiliar – similar things
could probably be said of Michael Jordan or Venus Williams). But,
like many difficult issues, this one turns on a problem of definition.
I'm only concerned with Beckham's day job, what he is able to do
on a football pitch. He can accomplish physical feats most other
people cannot; not only does he run some 16 km in the course of a
match, but he can kick a ball 60 metres to drop right into the path
of a running team mate. He can then move into an area of the
pitch where he might be able to receive the ball back; he can jink
and turn, and bend the ball around the goal keeper. Consider what
set of aptitudes are needed to be David Beckham. There are the
remarkable, but essentially uninteresting, levels of fitness,
suppleness, and strength. But there are also crucially a set of
anticipations of the nature of the physical and social aspects of the
game of football which are crucial both to the game and my
argument. When on form Beckham knows what will happen to the
ball when he kicks it with a particular velocity and part of his foot.
He is able to compensate for a heavy, soggy pitch or a windy day,
although he doesn't always get it right. Even more importantly he
can anticipate what his team mates and his opponents are doing
and will expect. When everything is going well, he can glance up

whilst running with the ball, take in the configuration of his own side and the opposition and play a ball that a highly experienced opposing team don't expect, but that someone on his team will. The fast-moving game of football blends a series of social and material skills seamlessly, all of which can be enacted on the instant, without the benefit of reflection. Training, of course, is vital. Many hours each day are spent kicking, running, and kicking again, to build up what is known as muscular memory: the muscles' ability to act in the proper sequence and with the right degree of delicacy and strength. Even a week or two off will make a player rusty. Tactics are also discussed. The strengths and weaknesses of the opposition, what happened last time and what can be learnt from the videos of previous games. But tactics are a minor part of the preparation, perhaps as important to give the team confidence that they are prepared and have a plan. It is the instantaneous action on the pitch, the fumbles, the brilliance, the surprises that turn the match.

Consider now the Boxgrove hominids, spears in hands, stalking the herd of horses (here we are moving rapidly over the line defining certain knowledge). They have a similar balance of the material and the social to get right if they are to hunt successfully. Crouched in the scrub around the open ground where the herd grazes they cannot each see all the other members of their group or all of the horses. They have to anticipate what others of their group and what the horses might do and this anticipation may have to be weighed in an instant. Once the group breaks cover to isolate a horse, they are running across broken ground, spears ready to be thrown, and they will not have long – this is a big, dangerous, fast horse. Individual prowess will help, but it is really essential that they all act together, knowing what the others are likely to do and adjusting their actions accordingly. Group action is the bedrock on which success is built. Like David Beckham—and many other sportsmen—their skills and intelligence are shown to best advantage when they are operating as part of a group.

These are all areas of life beyond words – the heft of a spear, the

32

allowing for wind and the swerving run of the horse – these things can be taught to some degree through verbal instructions, but can only be *learnt* through carrying them out. We can instruct children how to ride a bicycle, but they can only learn it for themselves, building up the right muscular memory, forms of balance, and understanding how hard you need to pedal up the big hill, not to mention the actions of drivers, pedestrians, and other cyclists. Much of our life is physical not verbal and involves a bodily understanding of the physical properties of objects and the social actions of others (these might be plants and animals as well as people). We can talk about riding a bicycle but never do full justice to the actual experience. Such skills are not something we know, but something that we are.

A Western view of intelligence emphasizes abstract thought. If Beckham were able to reduce the game of football to a series of equations describing the flight and velocity of the ball under different conditions, few would doubt his intelligence, although not many would pay to see him in action. The fact that he can actually make the ball fly in many different ways without the benefit of prior calculation does not fit within our definitions. But I would say that to know how the world works and how people operate within it forms the basis of our daily skills and intelligence and without these skills we would be something less than human.

As human beings we can do things and we can also think, talk, and write about what we have done, or even what we should have done, but didn't. Conventional views of intelligence emphasize the words in which we shape and express our thoughts as crucial. I am not trying to deny the importance of conscious thought or words, replacing this importance with action. Rather, the real mystery of human life lies in the intersection of habitual, but skilled action and conscious thought. Climbing onto my bike to ride to work in the morning, I'm rarely conscious of the bike itself, but am thinking about what has just happened at home, what is about to happen at work, and what I hope to do that day (or hope not to do). Only if the chain comes off the bike do I stop and pay attention to it, irritated at the oil on my hands and interruption to the flow of my thoughts. If I had to think about riding the bike, I could not give attention to the mass of other things that I consider to be really important. And my day, like everyone else's day, is made up of actions that require little conscious thought, along with a stream of actions that do, our attention flickering between the taken-for-granted world ('Why's that bloody printer so slow?') and what we need to give real conscious thought to ('How am I going to convince Jones that his thesis won't pass unless he puts in a lot more work?'). It is only when the taken-for-granted world poses a real problem (printer breaks at vital moment) or, more rarely, provides us with new and unexpected opportunities through working better than we had expected (Jones agrees immediately and goes off to the library, leaving me with a bonus three-quarters of an hour) that we need to give conscious thought to what we are doing.

Prehistory lacks words and seems impoverished as a result. Much of history lacks an understanding of habitual skilled action because the right sort of evidence has not been recorded, but people are less aware of this lack. To produce a handaxe you need thought about the shape of the nodule, the order in which you need to remove flakes for the handaxe shape to develop, and to modify your actions as the axe develops. The skill needed to strike the correct shape and size of flake is directly accessible from an analysis of the flakes by the archaeologist (providing they have the right skills). To reproduce the pattern of thought behind the handaxe is more difficult, involving more supposition, but is still possible.

At one time the boundary between humans and animals was thought to be formed by tool use. 'Man the toolmaker' had a series of technical skills that chimpanzees, gorillas, or monkeys lacked and this, it was thought, formed the basis of human evolution. From the 1960s Jane Goodall showed that chimps in Tanzania made tools from small twigs or grass to dip into termite mounds and fish out insects to eat. Chimps of the Ivory Coast and Liberia in West Africa spend over two hours a day cracking nuts open, using stones or branches to hit the nuts wedged into the roots of trees. Nut cracking is not easy and only adults can do it. The young are taught by their mothers how to make and use tools, but it takes some time to learn the skills. Good stone hammers are hidden near nut trees and chimps can remember a number of locations where hammers are hidden. Even more interestingly, not all chimp troupes in the Ivory Coast and Liberia crack nuts, even when the nut trees and suitable stone for hammers are found near each other. At some point in the history of a group an individual developed skills of nut cracking, passing it on to its young, but this did not happen in all groups. Different groups had their own histories and cultures. Other cultural differences between chimps have been observed with variations in the types of tools utilized for the same purpose in different areas. If chimps have technology in the wild, then the distinction with people breaks down. However, there is one really significant difference, I would argue: chimps never use material culture as the basis for their social relations; humans rarely create social relations without the use of material culture.

In his classic essay *The Gift* the French anthropologist Marcel Mauss called gift-giving in non-capitalist societies a 'total social fact', meaning that all human life could be traced to and from the obligations of give and take surrounding gifts. Mauss saw three obligations deriving from gifts – the obligation to give, the obligation to receive, and the obligation to repay. Certain situations oblige gifts (initiation rites, marriages, or deaths, as well as exchange partnerships set up for formalized exchanges). If I give you a gift, you cannot refuse it without seriously insulting me, and once you have taken it, repayment is required. Fine social judgement is needed as to when to repay (too soon looks like a refusal of the relationship, too late looks like you have forgotten or do not care), what to repay (the correct quality and amount of things must be finely judged), and with what degree of ceremony. Ongka, whom we met in the first chapter, was part of the ceremonial exchange systems of the New Guinea Highlands where pigs, shells, and in more recent years, beer, money, and Toyota Landcruisers, are given in great public ceremonies where the local Big Men proclaim their social power through practised rhetoric and their sense of theatre, as well as displaying the wealth they can afford to give away (a fine film *Ongka's Big Moka* was made of one such ceremonial transaction, part of a system of exchanges known locally as Moka). Sometimes identical exchanges are practised, such as axes for axes, and these forms of reciprocity show that it is the relationship that is important rather than the utility of the items being exchanged. Indeed, gift-giving has been termed a series of systems for creating social relations and is thus not straightforwardly economic in the sense that we would understand the term: people are exchanging to maintain contacts with others and (above all) to manipulate relationships of power, not to obtain things they need to live. Exchanges in many societies operate across a spectrum, from food sharing within the family, to regular, but socially unimportant, exchanges of food and other necessities within the group, to large ceremonial exchanges (or thefts) between groups. We have added market relations based around profit to such exchanges, but the exchange and accumulation of materials is still crucial to many social interactions. All social relations are at once material relations. For tool-using animals this is not true, with grooming, sex, and violence being the basis for most sociability. Food is shared, but little else is exchanged.

The Boxgrove hominids half a million years ago had technology of a sophisticated kind (way beyond anything that can be produced by chimps), but how far did they use this as the basis for their social life? We should not expect their sociability to look like our own, nor will it look like that of a chimp, leaving us to puzzle out what social life might have been like on the margins of southern Britain so long ago. One powerful recent theory outlining the basis of primate intelligence sees social life as crucial. Aiello and Dunbar have found a relationship between brain size and group size, so that the larger and more complex the group, the bigger the size of the brain (or, more accurately, the bigger the brain as a proportion of bodily size). This empirical relationship between brain and group size is thought to exist because the most complex area of a primate's life, and that which needs most thought, is the set of social relations in which they engage, which are much more complicated than dealing with the practical exigencies of the material world. Applying these ideas to human evolution we can see that the size of the brain has increased much more than we would expect simply on the basis of increased size of the body and in the last million years or so brain size has grown hugely, as has the complexity of its architecture, which is also very important. Aiello and Dunbar put this increase down to language. I would say that this is only part of the story and that language and material culture have both combined to give a complexity to hominid physical and mental skills that are unprecedented. Language is part of the change, but is not the only, or even the crucial, element. Tool use, as far as we know, started some 2.5 million years ago. The origins of language are still hotly debated, but are much more recent.

Prehistory is the history of social life and the sets of social and physical abilities that underpin our sociability, as indicated by material culture. To socialize we need certain skills and intelligence. Most other species that we would consider intelligent have well-developed patterns of sociability (primates, dolphins, and whales), but only humans develop their social life through two inextricable avenues at once, manipulating the physical world and the social world. To do this we have also combined a series of physical skills and mental abilities that are unique. Our lives have dual dimensions of the habitual and the thought, the things that we can do and our verbal abilities to think and talk. These are not opposed poles of thought and habit, but rather both make up our stream of consciousness in complex ways. We can think about how we ride a bicycle and come up with new and better ways to ride, but we can also ride and think about life, the universe, and everything, only being intermittently aware of cars, traffic lights, and pedestrians. We would love to know whether the skilled Boxgrove knapper chatted as she turned the flint nodule or worried silently about group relations, or the properties of different woods for making spears, or whether she had to give all her attention to the nodule itself, so that the rest of the world vanished in the act of knapping. Were handaxes or spears ever given as gifts? Were special cuts of meat given to particular people as they are in many modern societies? Did these hominids have words to worry with or to exchange? If none of these existed, when did human social life start, with its blend of thoughts and habits?

Becoming human

What does it mean to be human? I have just given one important element of the answer – we are the only animals to create our social life through things. Modern human beings share certain abilities. All live socially and their lives are shaped by the necessities of social obligations: they have to receive, to give, and to repay if they wish to remain members of society, although these obligations are given different cultural expressions. All use material culture to help create their social lives, not just through forms of exchange, but food, clothing, housing, and forms of wealth all create social personae of different kinds. All have non-verbal forms of expression through music and dance. All attempt to alter their consciousness and emotional states through drugs, trance, and dance. All human beings create and use language. These universals unite us all and make cross-cultural communication possible, despite the huge differences of cultural life around the planet. We presume, but don't really know, that such abilities have existed for the past 40,000 years. The longer history of what makes us human, going back to Boxgrove and way beyond, is increasingly murky, as are the exact trajectories of human life and difference on various parts of the planet.

So when did we become fully human? You will not be surprised to find that different answers are given to such a large question. The use of our bodies, the creation and manipulation of things and our

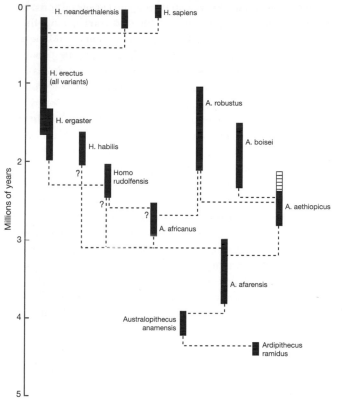

6. A family tree of hominid evolution over the last 5 million years

abilities with words are all vital to our sense of humanity and I shall look at each in turn.

The development of anatomically modern human bodies is becoming better known. Most people think that anatomically modern humans, *Homo sapiens sapiens*, first arose in Africa between 120,000 and 150,000 years ago, but even here there is controversy. The recent African origin model (recent in evolutionary terms that is!) holds that everyone in the world today descends from a common ancestral group in Africa and spread out from that continent a little less than 100,000 years ago into the Middle East and thence into Europe, Asia, and beyond. Modern humans encountered previous groups of humans, the best known of which are the Neanderthals (*Homo sapiens neanderthalensis*), a cold-adapted species found throughout Eurasia, and who probably descended from species like *Homo heidelbergensis*, the Boxgrove hominids. After a period of considerable overlap, especially in areas like the Middle East, the Neanderthals died out (whether they were wiped out by our ancestors or could not survive in the same landscape as them is unknown, but the subject of much speculation in TV programmes and novels), leaving us as the only hominid species. The competing hypothesis, known as the multi-regional model, holds that modern humans derive ultimately from populations of *Homo erectus* which moved out of Africa from about 1.8 million years ago onwards into Europe (probably), Asia, and south-east Asia, down to places like present-day Java. Supposed similarities in skull type, such as robust cheek bones, between *Homo erectus* fossils and modern-day Australian Aboriginal people lead to the conclusion of local evolution with only limited input from later incoming fully modern populations.

These two models, the recent African origin and the multi-regional hypothesis, like anything to do with human origins and diversity, each encourage different trains of thought about human unity, the nature of racial difference, and regional histories. The multi-regional hypothesis emphasizes human difference, raising the possibility that racial types, like those found in Europe and Asia, have long histories to them, making people and their histories separate and distinct. There are even dangers that by linking Aboriginal people to *Homo erectus*, an earlier human ancestor, they will be seen as 'primitive' in comparison to others, a view rife amongst 19th-century Europeans, but critiqued today (see Chapter 4). There is a considerable range of evidence, mainly fossil and genetic evidence, against the multi-regional hypothesis, although its advocates are still stubborn in its defence. If we all derive from

African populations we would expect Africans to be more diverse genetically than the rest of us, which appears true, and for modern human genetic variability outside Africa to represent a subset of African genetic lineages. Not only does it appear that we are descended from a common ancestor from Africa, but that all human genes outside Africa probably derive from lineages found in present-day Somalia and Ethiopia, exactly where we would expect humans migrating out of the continent to be found. Taken as a whole, human genetic variability is very low, much less than that found within chimps or gorillas. The differences of skin colour, hair, and face shape, which some people make so much of, are controlled by very few genes and tend to mask a much deeper human unity. Equally important as evidence against the multi-regional hypothesis is the fact that the recovery of ancient DNA from three different Neanderthal skeletons in Europe and the Caucasus indicates no genetic link between ourselves and Neanderthals, making it very unlikely that they are the ancestors of present-day Europeans, all of whom derive from the African migrants, as must be true for the rest of the globe. Last, but by no means least, the earliest fossils of fully modern humans are found in Africa, only turning up later elsewhere and this may also be true of some types of stone tools associated with our own direct ancestors.

For most prehistorians, a recent African origin for fully modern humans is the only means to make sense of the evidence we have. A more difficult, partly philosophical, question is when did we become behaviourally human? I assume that if it were possible to clone a fully modern human from 100,000 years ago, put them in modern dress, suitably washed and coiffured, and sit them on a bus no one would pick them out as physically different. But they might well behave oddly. Even our earliest fully modern ancestor would have been much the same height, weight, and brain size as the rest of us, their arms and legs worked in the same way, as did their eyes, ears, and brain. But possessing the same physical and mental abilities as ourselves does not mean that they would have learnt to use them in the same way. And here we return to a crucial element of my argument. All fully modern humans, of whatever time and place, have the same capacity for culture as ourselves, but may not have learnt or needed to exercise that capacity. Being fully human is not just about the capability of the body, but about the links between the body and the material world which have developed the capabilities of the body in lots of different ways. In the present all humans have close links with other plant and animal species, as well as with lots of material things, and these relationships have developed over many millennia. We could take our cloned ancestor off the bus and teach them to ride a bicycle, but this would involve them in learning physical and social skills, necessary for them to stay up and to anticipate what drivers and pedestrians were going to do, which they did not originally have and thus extending themselves in new ways. Human history is about the extension of the inherent capacities of the body through actual use, and because various cultures have different needs and values human bodies are given different skills and develop various capabilities. I remember a chastening experience in Papua New Guinea trying to learn to windsurf together with a local guy who had sailed in canoes all his life, who had a sense of balance, and an understanding of manœuvring a sail that I entirely lacked. Whereas he stepped onto the windsurfer and made immediate, satisfying progress across the bay, I spent all my time pulling the sail out of the water, falling straight back in, and complaining that the wind was too strong for a beginner. The gap in our abilities greatly enhanced his enjoyment of the experience.

A crucial lesson for the prehistorian to learn is to avoid anachronism: not to assume that the world of the past is too like that of the present, that just because fully modern humans could potentially do all the things that we can that they actually did so. It thus becomes an empirical matter to decide when *Homo sapiens sapiens* started to use their capabilities in a manner we would recognize as fully modern human in a social and cultural sense. The general answer given to this is between 60,000 and 20,000 years ago, with the transition between the Middle and the Upper

Palaeolithic. This, as Clive Gamble has written, involved 'the Other becoming Us'. Gamble also feels that the main change is a growing freedom from the immediacies of life, so that time and space become socially extended. Boxgrove hominids made beautiful handaxes, demonstrating considerable skill in producing artefacts of great utility and considerable aesthetic appeal (to us and possibly to them). These handaxes were made from material obtained locally and were often dropped very close to where they had been used. Making stone tools in the Upper Palaeolithic (40,000–10,000 BC) came to involve getting stone from considerable distances, up to several hundred kilometres, and longer chains of action to make things, as well as people keeping, using, and exchanging things for longer. Social interaction and the use of material culture to build social links were not just about the here and now in the Upper Palaeolithic, but artefacts came to take on some of the values attached to places and significant others. A convincing definition of a symbol is 'something which stands for something else' – the colour red for blood or the word 'cat' for the animal. Ivory and bone are carved into the shapes of people and animals and so-called Venus figurines are made from clay and stone. The Sunghir necklace, found on a site in northern Russia at the height of the last glacial (around 18,000 years ago) was made from 3,000 individual beads and must have enhanced or changed the social standing of the wearer in some manner (Figure 5).

In the Upper Palaeolithic artefacts take on significances beyond the here and now, extending people's chains of social connection over space and across time. Material culture and social relations are intimately linked, so that one could not exist in the same form without the other. Places and people were probably imbued with meanings and emotional responses as never before.

Meaning and symbolism do not just adhere to things, but are also bound up with language, the last major element of modern humanity. There is considerable controversy as to when human language started, whether with the Neanderthals (or even earlier)

Human skills and experiences

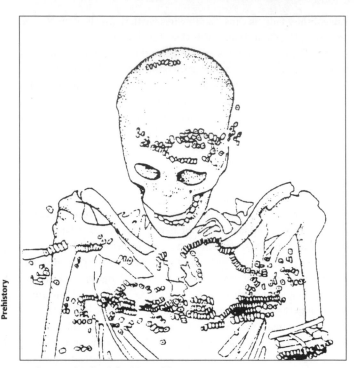

5. The Sunghir burial with necklace

or with the fully moderns. Attempts to teach chimpanzees to speak in the 1960s foundered on the fact that chimps lack the right architecture of the mouth and throat to create the range of sounds that we can. They were thus unable to speak at all well. Once the researchers switched to sign language, however, things changed, so that both chimps and gorillas were able to demonstrate sophisticated concepts about themselves, others, the material world, the past, and the future through signing. Much discussion of Neanderthal language has concerned whether they could vocalize in the same manner as ourselves, a discussion held back by the lack of much direct evidence on throat length, tongue, or palate. Even if they could not speak, Neanderthals could probably communicate through a range of actions and sounds. But the question really turns not only physical abilities, but on social needs. The longer, deeper chains of action involving extended and deep relations between people and things over time and space seem to be lacking for the Middle Palaeolithic. Neanderthal societies, for whatever reason, restrained the need to develop sophisticated forms of linguistic communication. Neanderthals may not have felt the need to engage in discussions of the type of 'Remember that mammoth we killed five years ago, I'm still using one of its bones to knap flint with', whereas a fully modern human might have said 'I treasure this bow, because it was made for me by my mother using the sinews of a mammoth she helped kill five years ago'. Of course we will never know the emotional attachments of either species but suspect a greater range and depth of attachments to people and things from the Upper Palaeolithic than for any previous period and a greater ability to express these attachments verbally. Deep attachments to artefacts and to people derived both from the things themselves and their significances, but also from words spoken about people and things. This sets up a tension between the habitual, taken-for-granted areas of life, which we feel but cannot speak, and words which directly, if partially, express what people feel. It is this tension between words and action that is crucial to our lives and may not have existed for any other species.

Full humanity arose through a special combination of bodily abilities, the world of things and the dimension of language, all of which combined in modern form for the first time around 40,000 years ago.

David Beckham is certainly no word-smith, but he does display vital elements of human intelligence in abundance, combining the physical and the social on the football pitch in ways that few others can manage. As Sarah Bernhardt said: 'If I could talk it, I wouldn't need to dance.' Dance would not see itself as an art form which is poorer than theatre, but something quite different. Football is a form of theatre created through actions, which can only inadequately be described by the commentator. Prehistory concerns performances, mundane and spectacular, and the uses of the human body in creating worlds that make sense to us, which we belatedly try to capture in words. The variety of those worlds, past and present, is one of the things that draws us to study human society and culture, so that the nature of variety and difference lies at the heart of the puzzles of prehistory.

Chapter 4
Continental prehistories

In this chapter I shall explore the possibility that each continent has its own form of prehistory. There is evidence, as I shall outline, that the populations of each continent go back 15,000 years, without massive additions in later periods. This continuity of people may form the basis for a continuity of culture and history, even in fairly ephemeral areas of life like mythology. If this argument for long-term continuity holds water (and it is contentious), it means that what has generally been seen as the big change in human prehistory, the invention of farming, does not herald great population increases or movements, nor a rapid and fundamental alteration in all areas of people's lives. In this chapter I shall look first at the genetic evidence for population continuity, deriving from the processes of global colonization and the influence of the last glaciation, then critically review the evidence for large migrations of people due to population increases after farming developed and then consider new ways of thinking about the co-dependencies between people, plants and animals which have varying manifestations on each continent. Putting forward a novel interpretation like this is risky and many other prehistorians will disagree with it, not least due to interpretations of the evidence. However, to emphasize differences between continents also has implications for human unity and diversity.

Archaeologists and anthropologists have taken two basic routes to understanding human variety and unity. The first derives from the social evolutionary approaches of the mid-19th century where our similarity as a species was stressed and effort was directed towards understanding how humanity as a whole progressed through stages like hunting and gathering, farming, the development of states, and, most importantly, civilization. Social Darwinists, so-called, ranging from Herbert Spencer to Pitt Rivers and E. B. Tylor, struck by the force of Darwin's views, were attracted by the possibility of a single theoretical basis for approaches to the humanities, which also chimed with their desire to found archaeology and ethnology as sciences. The 'onwards and upwards' view of prehistory was predicated on a belief in progress, implicit in which was the idea that not everyone progressed at the same rate or to the same degree. Only those of European descent made it through the full gamut of historical stages to become rational, civilized, democratic, and energetic, leaving less progressive others in their wake, still remnants of earlier stages of world history, in the form of Australian aboriginal people, African peasant farmers, or the more 'static' civilizations of various parts of Asia.

It is not hard to see why progressive and unitary views of human life were unattractive to many, including some of European descent.

At the beginning of the 20th century, an alternative set of views was promulgated by Boas in America, but working from the intellectual framework of a German tradition which emphasized the local specificity and integrity of human cultures. Culture was later to be defined by the archaeologist Gordon Childe as a constantly recurring set of traits, such as artefacts, houses, burials, food, and so on, behind which lay similarities harder to discern archaeologically such as of kinship, language, and customs. These cultural historical views saw the world as a mosaic of cultural forms, each with their habits of life, ways of seeing the world, and histories. Each culture could only be understood in its own terms and it was variety that was characteristic of human life, not unity. Bruce Trigger's view of

8. Triumphalist evolution

the history of archaeological thought is one of alternation between
approaches stressing unity, such as the early evolutionary
approaches of the later 19th century, which made a resurgence
between the 1950s and 1970s, and those stressing difference. Boas's
and Childe's culture-historical views, emphasizing different local
historical trajectories, made something of a come-back in the 1980s
as postmodernist thought raised doubts about the scientific
ambitions of an evolutionary archaeology, and made a broader

critique of a possible Western objective viewpoint, stressing the need to understand other forms of life in their own terms.

Today our questions have shifted away from why some people did not ascend to the top rung of the ladder of progress and towards how people created worlds for themselves that made internal sense. Indeed, many now question whether these local worlds can be encompassed by a single scheme, especially one developed to make sense of the European past. Also, an emphasis on technological change has been replaced (for some at least) by an enquiry into how people construct worlds for themselves through putting together varying skills and techniques, developing particular sets of social, physical, and intellectual skills in the process. Human beings have a huge range of potentials; cultural forms and histories involve developing some of these skills but neglecting others. Australian Aboriginal people were described as the virtuosos of the human mind by the anthropologist Lévi-Strauss because of the huge amount of genealogical and cosmological knowledge they developed and maintained, putting much less emphasis on the creation and use of material things. A set of cultural forms in which knowledge is power challenges the prehistoric archaeologist whose main evidence is artefacts. But it does alert us to the idea that cultures cannot be measured along a single axis, as more or less complex, still less better or worse, but rather as being different. Cross-cultural comparison is necessary, but to bring out contrasts with others, not to measure everyone with the same yardstick.

The tension between difference and unity has always been crucial to writing prehistory. I am attempting here a tricky act of balance in saying that there are things that all human beings share, but that there are differences which divide us. To help understand what I am trying to do, let us look briefly at language. All human groups have languages. Children in human society learn language spontaneously: we can encourage them in this learning, but it is not a process that adults need to initiate; it happens anyway. The so-called Sapir–Whorf hypothesis (which is controversial within linguistics) holds that language is not just the means through which we express our thoughts and feelings about the world, but the means through which we develop those thoughts and feelings. If languages, as forms of conceptual apparatus, differ around the globe, people will not just talk and write about the world in their own way, they will actually inhabit their own worlds of thought, feeling, and belief. So, we could put two different language groups in the same environment, English speakers and Aboriginal Australians for instance, and that environment would not be the same at all. This is an experiment that colonial history has played out, at enormous cost to Aboriginal people. We know that the two groups do attend to different aspects of the world: whites are interested in metal resources, the possibilities for grazing sheep and growing wheat, not to mention the qualities of surf and sea; Aboriginal people live in a totemic landscape, created by ancestral figures in the Dreamtime, who shaped the rocks, rivers, deserts, plants, and animals, which need to be cared for as much as exploited. As I have stressed previously, people do not just live linguistically, but through patterns of skilled action in the world, and they do not perceive the world passively but rather through their patterns of action which shape the world, as it shapes them. Human unity resides in our ability to build relations with one another through the medium of material things and in our ability to create language. Everywhere also there is some tension between language and action, which lies at the heart of what it means to be human. Languages, human beings, and cultural forms all have their own more local histories, which unfold at a number of levels, from the continental to the truly local, and it is the role of the continents in creating human difference out of unity that I want to explore here.

To emphasize the depth of human difference in a temporal and cultural sense is a dangerous and possibly irresponsible act in a world where much fear and distrust are accruing around people who aren't quite like us. Saying that the variety of languages, customs, beliefs, thoughts, and feelings have long and deep histories to them might make those differences appear unbridgeable. There is no doubt that distrust can derive from difference. Equally, all of us are capable of acts of sympathetic understanding that allow us, to some degree, to enter into and live in other people's worlds. The spirit of our enquiry is crucial, which, if it starts from the need for inter-cultural communication, can lead us to explore the history of human variability and, while not attempting to overcome, deny, or do away with otherness, we can see it as an incitement and a challenge which will necessitate us (whoever we are) expanding our conceptual universe and human sensibilities. Ultimately, for me the study of prehistory has this as an admittedly utopian goal.

How, why, where, and when do the continents differ in their prehistories? To start to answer such a daunting raft of questions let us go back to the history of human colonization we left in the last chapter. The only primate species living on all the continents is *Homo sapiens sapiens*. The expansion of humans is unique and has only been completed over the last 15,000 years or less (Figure 9).

In Chapter 3, we saw that our modern human ancestors arose in Africa some 120,000 years ago, leaving that continent 90,000 years ago and spreading through Europe and Asia by 40,000 BC. A most amazing part of this expansion was the movement into Australia and New Guinea, at least 40,000 years ago (and possibly as long ago as 60,000 BC – dates are controversial). Although Australia and Papua New Guinea were joined at periods of lower sea level into the giant landmass known as Sahul until 6000 BC, this landmass has always been separated by sea from the island archipelago of present-day Indonesia. The biologist Wallace, a contemporary of Darwin's who came up with a theory of biological change similar to the theory of evolution, recognized the huge differences in plants and animals between south-east Asia and Australia. The Wallace Line divides the placental mammals (monkeys, elephants, tigers, etc.) of south-east Asia from the marsupials of Sahul. The history of continental drift created the super-continent of Wallacea

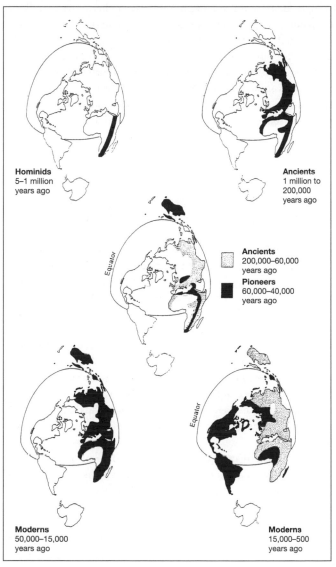

Hominids
5–1 million
years ago

Ancients
1 million to
200,000
years ago

Equator

Ancients
200,000–60,000
years ago

Pioneers
60,000–40,000
years ago

Equator

Moderns
50,000–15,000
years ago

Moderns
15,000–500
years ago

9. The process of global colonization

(composed of Antarctica, South America, southern Africa, India, and Sahul) on which marsupials developed and then broke it up, so that Antarctica drifted south and froze, killing all animal life, and all the other continental fragments bumped into other continents (North America, northern Africa, and Asia) which had large, carnivorous animals which promptly ate all the marsupials. Australia reached its present position some 10 million years ago and remained isolated enough by the northern seas to deter the entry of placental mammals.

Humans were the first species to cross this major biogeographical barrier and entered a world of plants (the gums, acacias, etc.) and animals completely new to them. Such novelty was increased by the latitudinal range of Sahul which stretched from the Equator to sub-Antarctic regions of southern Tasmania, including the Highlands of New Guinea, the highest mountains east of the Himalayas and the massive central deserts. Sahul represents a laboratory for testing out modern human capabilities, tests which our ancestors passed with ease, so that by 40,000 years ago there were groups hunting up by glaciers in central Tasmania, in the temperate zones of south-eastern and south-western Australia, well into the desert, and all over the tropical north. Not long afterwards they reached islands off present-day Papua New Guinea, where I have spent some time digging caves, which have revealed some of the earliest marine fishing in the world and evidence of island occupation much earlier than any of the other island groups of the world, such as the Mediterranean or the Caribbean.

Given the date and apparent ease with which people moved into and through Sahul, the occupation of the Americas poses a considerable puzzle. There has been more controversy over the human history of the Americas than any other continent. There have been claims of occupation 80,000 years ago or more, but these are not the really controversial ones because they lack an empirical basis. Given that people entered the Americas from Siberia it is surprising that there are two sites in South America, Pedra Furada in Brazil and Monte Verde in Chile, which may be older than any found in north America, possibly first used by people 30,000 years ago. Monte Verde, in south–central Chile, has an undoubted occupation of an open-air site 13,000 years ago, with evidence preserved in a peat bog of log foundations for huts, a piece of mastodon flesh, a human footprint, animal skins, plant remains, wooden and stone tools (Figure 10).

This sedentary occupation has brought into question the notion that early inhabitants were mobile hunter-gatherers, and the site shows trade links with other groups. But the possibility that there might be an occupation some 20,000 years older is controversial and troubling, and one that Tom Dillehay, the excavator of the site, seems increasingly doubtful about: below the main layers are a possible hearth and possible tools dating to 30,000 BP, the qualifications receiving greater emphasis as time goes by. Pedra Furada in eastern Brazil has produced dates between 32,000 and 17,000 years ago. There is considerable scepticism (especially amongst North American archaeologists) about these dates, as the charcoal dated may come from natural fires and the stone tools may have been created when stones on the top of the cliff above the site were washed down, suffering natural fractures mimicking those produced by people. Of course, pride is involved here. Huge effort has been expended in North America to find very early sites, with no generally accepted results. There may be more professional archaeologists in North America than in much of the rest of the world put together and it is hard for all these highly skilled professionals to accept that there might be early sites out there that they have failed to find. And as our common sense would indicate that people entered the continent from the north we would expect a cline of dates from north to south, not the reverse.

In 1932 large blade tools were found near the town of Clovis, New Mexico, in association with the bones of extinct animals. Clovis points have now been found in every state of the Union, up into the Arctic Circle, and deep into South America.

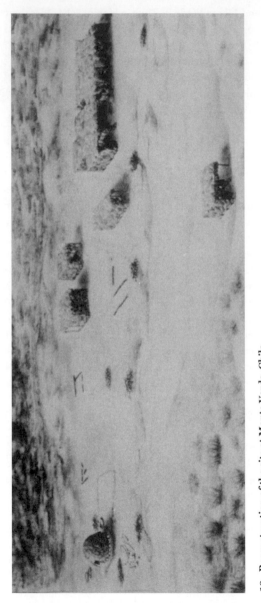

10. Reconstruction of the site at Monte Verde, Chile

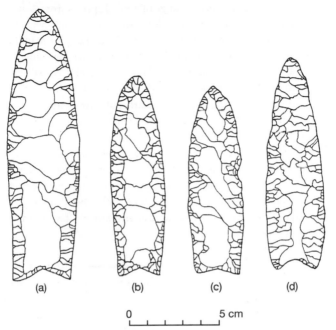

(a)   (b)   (c)   (d)

0   5 cm

11. Typical Clovis blades

Radiocarbon dates place these sites at 12,000 years ago, with another horizon of Folsom points about 2,000 years later. Clovis represents the first undoubted occupation of the continent and at this time the continent was inhabited by a series of so-called megafauna, such as mammoths, sabre-toothed tigers, giant moose, and a species of beaver, the size of a modern bear, making the continent very attractive to hunters. It seems most sensible that people walked into the continent from present-day Siberia, which was inhabited from at least 23,000 years ago, with distributions of leaf-shaped points covering north-eastern Siberia, Alaska, and western Canada by 15,000 years ago. Glaciations producing periods of lower sea level have created a land bridge across the Bering Sea (so-called Beringia) at least four times in the last 60,000 years and this has led to migrations of a range of animal species from Asia to America. Humans may have been deterred by the relative paucity of game in Beringia itself, a relatively barren area, and the size of the ice-sheets across Alaska. Alternatively they may have gone down the coast, travelling by sea, as did the first entrants into Australia, which would make some sense of early dates in somewhere like Monte Verde. I would be happy with early dates from South America, but accept that the present evidence is not overwhelming. On the basis of the distributions of leaf-shaped points down into eastern Canada and the fact that the 13,000-year-old occupation at Monte Verde does not look like the initial stages of colonization, I would opt for an initial date of some 15,000 years ago for the first colonization of the Americas, leaving time for the build-up of population which led to the widespread visibility of Clovis sites, some 3,000 years later.

Such a date allows interesting parallels to be drawn with Eurasia. Although fully modern humans entered south-west Asia more than 90,000 years ago and moved thence into Europe, there is increasing evidence, from Europe especially, that during the last glacial maximum down to some 14,500 years ago, people retreated to places like northern Spain–southern France and the Balkans–Ukraine areas, along with a whole range of other animal and plant species, only to recolonize the continent once temperatures started to rise. Intriguing recent genetic evidence shows that 80 per cent of Europeans can trace their lineage through their mother's line back to populations that were in Europe some 14,000 years ago, with only 20 per cent of mitochondrial lineages coming in more recently. The surprise contained in such a result is because many felt that the development of farming at around 10,000 years ago would have caused a rise in population levels, due to more secure food supplies, leading to expansions of populations from early centres of agriculture (such as the Near East in the Eurasian case, but also China, Central America, South America, and Highland Papua New Guinea) out in all directions to overwhelm the low-density hunter-gatherer groups.

The evidence for the history of languages becomes relevant here, primarily through the work of Colin Renfrew. In 1796, Sir William Jones, chief justice of India and founder of the Royal Asiatic Society, presented a famous discourse on Indian culture in which he pointed out the similarities between the ancient language of India, Sanskrit, and numerous other languages, such as Persian, Greek, Latin, the Germanic, and Celtic languages, found across Europe and Asia.

The word for fire, for instance, is *agnis* in Sanskrit and *ignis* in Latin, from which English takes the word 'ignite'. All the languages of Europe (with a few exceptions, such as Basque, Hungarian, Estonian, and Finnish), some Asian languages, such as Armenian, Persian, and a large number of Indian languages, have been grouped together and termed 'Indo-European' languages. Jones sought an origin for these languages in the diaspora thought to have happened after Noah's ark had landed, which is not an origin many would accept today. However, a great deal of effort has gone into reconstructing an Indo-European proto-language on the basis of similarities in the forms of words known today and systematic changes in their word form over time. The surprising, but undeniable, basis of historical linguistics is the fact that there are systematic sound changes between one language and another, for instance *ph* in Greek regularly becomes *b* in Germanic languages – thus the Greek *phrater*, 'clan member', becomes English *brother*. Systematic changes allow connections to be made and histories to be reconstructed

In the 1980s, almost 200 years after William Jones, Renfrew became interested in whether the origins of the Indo-Europeans could be linked to changes in the archaeological evidence. Indeed, Renfrew looked forward to a 'grand synthesis' of archaeology, historical linguistics, and genetics. In considering the distribution of Indo-European languages he felt that there was only one episode or process over the last few thousand years that could be

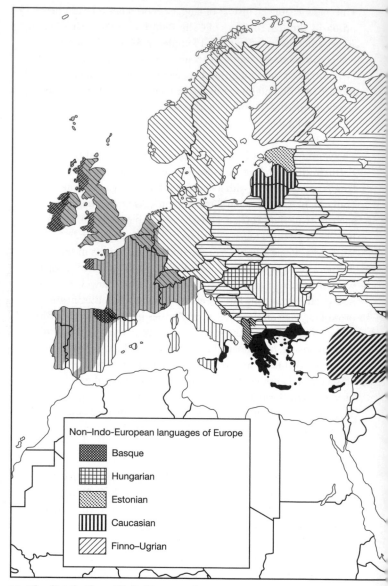

12. The distribution of Indo-European languages

Non–Indo-European languages of Europe
- Basque
- Hungarian
- Estonian
- Caucasian
- Finno–Ugrian

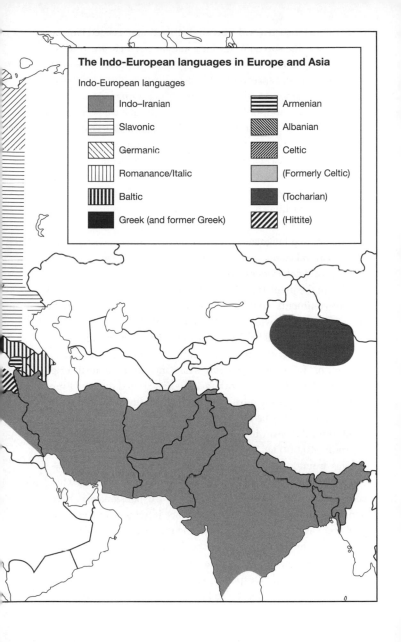

The Indo-European languages in Europe and Asia

Indo-European languages

- Indo–Iranian
- Slavonic
- Germanic
- Romanance/Italic
- Baltic
- Greek (and former Greek)
- Armenian
- Albanian
- Celtic
- (Formerly Celtic)
- (Tocharian)
- (Hittite)

responsible for such a widespread distribution of related languages and that was the spread of farming and farmers. He and others subsequently broadened the farming-origins hypothesis to account for the origins and spread of other broadly distributed language groups, chief amongst which were the Niger–Congo group of western, central and southern Africa thought to have been carried from west Africa by the migration of Bantu agriculturalists and the Austronesian languages found throughout south-east Asia (with an outlier in Madagascar), the coastal languages of Papua New Guinea and the Solomons and out into the Pacific as far as Hawai'i, Easter Island, and New Zealand, thought to be spread by farmers originally from Taiwan.

The theory that language spread through farming was only one among several competing hypotheses. It was formulated in advance of much evidence from modern molecular genetics and led to the prediction that early farmers expanding across the various continents would leave a clear genetic signal. The genetic results have not provided much evidence of Neolithic migration and Renfrew himself has been one of the first to acknowledge this fact. The overwhelming continuity of populations from the Palaeolithic in Europe necessitates new models of linguistic origin and spread, unconnected with farming. The populations of Europe may long pre-date the advent of farming, as shown by the lack of genetic input in the last 10,000 years, but also do not show continuity all the way back to the first advent of modern humans at around 40,000 BC. The expansion of people out of their glacial refuges around 15,000 years ago gives the majority of people in Europe a similar length of history to those in the Americas who colonized for the first time then. The same expansions may have happened in Asia, although our evidence is not yet good enough. And there are arguments for Australia that people were driven into refuges by the expansion of the deserts, to re-emerge from 15,000 years ago, although again present evidence is sparse. Contractions and then expansions of populations of people with the last glacial cycle might also have occurred in Africa. If such expansions occurred (and it is still a big if), on all continents, the populations trace their ancestry back to the end of the last Ice Age. Although there have been more recent population movements, these have been surprisingly local and minor, prior to the last 500 years.

Is it possible that the distribution of Indo-European languages first occurred in the late Palaeolithic when there are widespread similarities in material culture across wide areas of Eurasia, to be reinforced and to some extent reordered by later contacts? This is a proposal that would make sense of the genetics, not conflict with archaeological evidence, but find little support amongst linguists (partly because anything occurring so long ago is beyond the range of historical reconstruction). But it must be said that no proposal so far has pleased a majority in all three disciplines. Similarly, in the Austronesian area, indications from genetics don't show evidence of a homeland in Taiwan, the proximate origin of farming groups, but in eastern Indonesia, where there is no particular evidence of origins of farming. The links between language, genetics, and archaeology look anything but clear-cut and the hypothesis of farming spreads is not bearing up well, even in Africa where the Bantu migrations are not accepted by some archaeologists and the genetic evidence is not well understood, but obviously very complicated. The Australian languages are not related to any outside the continent (the only possible exception being those of the Highlands of New Guinea), indicating some ancient divergence between them and all other language families. The languages of the Americas are still surprisingly controversial. Na-Dene languages of North America form a tight group, presumably due to recent origins, but many of the languages of the rest of the continent are lumped, rather than grouped in any typological sense, and their unity is very dubious.

Prehistory has no words to offer us directly, but language is not totally beyond the scope of historical reconstruction based on the distribution of similarities and differences between recent languages. The same process of inference, moving from the distribution of modern traits to deeper histories, is found in genetics, where the recovery and analysis of DNA from ancient skeletons is still fraught with all sorts of difficulties. The analysis of modern genetic traits is producing a picture from all the continents of stable and ancient populations with marked continuities through to the present. The major proviso here is the massive replacement of indigenous populations by Europeans in places like North America, Australia, and New Zealand. Populations were well established in all continents by the late Pleistocene and have remained mainly stable since then, with relatively few incomers prior to the last 500 years. Genes best demonstrate long-term continuities, supported by archaeological evidence. The historical situation for languages is still debated. However, the general evidence for continuity over the last 15,000 years provides the basis for positing differences in the prehistory for each of the continents.

Throughout the world the expansion of people due to the start of farming has not received strong support from genetics or archaeology, making us turn to longer term histories. It has also contributed to an on-going re-think about the nature and start of farming itself.

Commensualism

Commensualism denotes a process of living together in mutual support and dependency. Modern human life involves close relations with particular plants, animals and material things. We depend in Europe on cereals, cows and sheep for food, but in their domesticated forms they depend on us for propagation, nurture and survival. Such mutual links often developed gradually, rather than being invented suddenly. The use of particular animals or plants as foods encourages special forms of material culture for cooking and consumption, so that long relations with other species may encourage special sets of tools for conviviality in the form of pots, stone tools, ovens or houses. Living together with plants or animals involves the creation of new landscapes each with their own patterns of fields and woods, or deserts and wadis, or rainforests with clearings. Commensualism is a process whereby people create worlds for themselves with special structures of community, landscapes and artefacts, as well as their own forms of histories. Local landscapes can be created through local developments, but much has also moved and diffused between populations over the last 10,000 years.

In various continents people share linked histories of mutual dependency with plant and animal species. Cattle and sheep herds were vulnerable to predation and disease without human skill and care; domesticated cereals find it hard to penetrate the ground surface and cannot seed without human help; apples, beans, or carrots only propagate with difficulty on their own. Dense human populations needed these species to maintain themselves. Less obvious but equally important were the close commensuals, such as rats, birds, insects, and intestinal worms which lived in houses, fields, and the human body and whose histories became completely entangled with humans. Commensualism also exists as forms of power between women and men, adults and children, the spirit and the human worlds, and those central to the group and those on its edge. Last, but most important, commensualism is about aesthetics and emotions, the sensual operations of the body which attach values to things and to people forming the bedrock of shared belief. It goes without saying that life was not identical in all areas of all continents, but each continent had its own special range of variations of commensualism, its own band-width of responses.

As Jared Diamond has pointed out, it is easier to form links across the same latitude due to similarities in vegetation, temperature, day-length, and seasonality than it is north–south across the grain of a landmass. The steppe regions from the Ukraine to northern China have more similarities with each other in a physical sense than they do with the forested regions to the north or the deserts to their south and this may have promoted travel, contact, and the movement of plants, animals, and trade products along the grain of the continent – the Silk Route through the deserts, with its Bronze Age origins, is the most famous example of such a set of connections. Eurasia has seen complex transfers of technology and resources over the last millennia, making it impossible to divide Europe from Asia. On all continents introductions from elsewhere are important, but new crops or items of material culture were only accepted if they found a place within older schemes of life.

An important element holding people together is food. There was an important shift in emphasis during the 20th century in thoughts about food, a movement from an emphasis on production to that on consumption. Gordon Childe thought that there were three big revolutions in human history – the Neolithic, the Urban, and the Industrial – and both life in towns, first occurring 3500 BC, and recent industrialization were eventual outcomes of the adoption of farming, which was thus the crucial moment. The Neolithic was revolutionary for Childe because the adoption of domesticated plants and animals provided a greater security in food supplies, allowing for control over the environment, rather than life as a hunter-gatherer at its mercy. The production of a secure food supply allowed people to settle down and a sedentary life provided the need and the leisure to produce more varied and sophisticated material culture, such as pottery, textiles, ground stone, and houses, with later experiments in metal technology. 'The escape from the impasse of savagery was an economic and scientific revolution that made the participants active partners with nature instead of parasites upon nature' (Childe 1942: 48). Farmers not only altered nature through domestication of plants and animals, but also 'created new substances which do not occur ready-made in nature' (Childe 1942: 49). Pottery, wool, and flax were concrete manifestations of a more rational appreciation of nature and its properties. A further innovation of Childe's thought was to bring in a gendered aspect. 'All the foregoing inventions [various agricultural techniques, brewing, etc.] were, judged by ethnographic evidence, the work of women. To that sex, too, may by the same token be credited the chemistry of pot-making, the physics of spinning, the mechanics of the loom and the botany of flax and cotton' (Childe 1942: 59). The Neolithic revolution could not have been more profound, altering people's relationships with nature and with each other. All the innovations Childe highlighted concerned production, containing the assumption that the advantages of his various inventions were so self-evident that they would be immediately adopted.

We can now see that moves towards farming were often not sudden, nor did they represent a complete break with prior ways of life. Let us take an extended look at one site from the Near East, the area which for Childe was the cradle of much of Eurasian farming. The earliest plant and animal domestication took place in western Asia, the area from eastern Turkey to the Levant. In northern Syria on the middle Euphrates is a large lake behind a dam. Beneath the waters of the lake lies a site known as Abu Hureyra, excavated in the 1970s prior to the construction of the dam. The inhabitants of the site would have had access to a great range of foodstuff and raw materials, including plants and animals from the wet valley of the Euphrates and a nearby wadi, those of the forest steppe, and slightly further away from the open-park woodland of the hills. There are two superimposed settlements at Abu Hureyra; one in which people supplemented hunting and gathering with growing crops and a second where crops and domesticated animals became more important. The site was first occupied 11,500 years ago by people who hunted gazelle.

Each spring herds of Persian gazelle moved north from their wintering grounds in southern Syria, through the El Kum pass, and on to the Euphrates. Abu Hureyra was sited just where they turned west to fan out across the steppe and the coming of the gazelle would have been the vital point in the inhabitants' lives for almost 3,000 years.

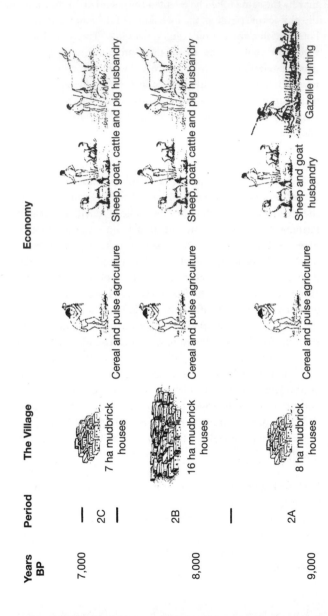

Years BP	Period	The Village	Economy		
7,000	2C	7 ha mudbrick houses	Cereal and pulse agriculture	Sheep, goat, cattle and pig husbandry	
8,000	2B	16 ha mudbrick houses	Cereal and pulse agriculture	Sheep, goat, cattle and pig husbandry	
9,000	2A	8 ha mudbrick houses	Cereal and pulse agriculture	Sheep and goat husbandry	Gazelle hunting

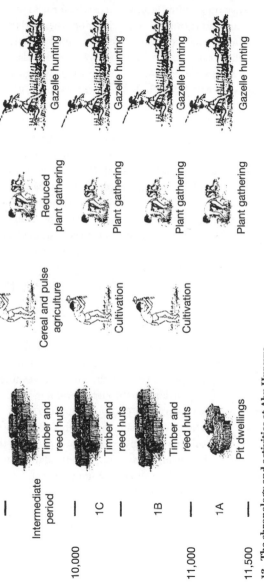

13. **The chronology and activities at Abu Hureyra**

The inhabitants of the site lived in timber and reed huts, and made flint and bone tools and grinding stones and pestles for wild plant processing. From around 11,000 years ago, a period when the warm conditions of the late glacial gave way to a colder, wetter climate, people started to grow domestic rye and possibly other cereals; the increase in weed seeds associated with cultivation are a good indirect indicator of field cultivation. Between 11,500 and 9,000 years ago people's lives probably had a strong seasonal round. In April the coming of the gazelle herds would have meant an intensive period of slaughter, butchery, and possible salting or storage of some of the meat. This was also a time when many wild grasses needed to be gathered and by June the domestic rye needed harvesting. The onset of high summer between July and November meant there were millet and club-rush seeds to be gathered in the valley bottom and grasses, roots and tubers on the steppe, along with more casual hunting of deer and pigs. There is some evidence that more women than men processed plant foods, as wear on the bones of the back and the feet indicated heavy grinding in a kneeling position; some men also took part in this work. Between December and April roots and tubers were gathered and some hunting took place.

The gradual introduction of domesticated plants and animals added to this cycle rather than supplanted it. The soil would have been prepared and the crop planted during the summer; weeding and general care of the crop took place through the winter, with harvest and processing in the spring. By 10,000 years ago there were perhaps 300 people living on the site, making this a settlement of a new type. There are continuities through this early period in the flint and bone tools used, showing some stability in the daily round. Hearth placement within huts also stayed the same, so that generation after generation orientated themselves around their fire in a similar manner. It is clear that large-scale sedentism preceded agriculture and that agriculture did not come as a sudden invention, but as a series of additions that fitted into and extended a prior pattern of life. The structure of the year provided the pattern for growing and harvesting crops, like rye. Those crops produced seeds which could be made into the same sorts of porridges and breads that wild seeds were used for, so that continuity of tasks and of consumption eased the passage of novelty into existing ways of life. People, animals, and plants grew together over many generations, the habits and needs of each becoming apparent to the others.

Nevertheless, Abu Hureyra is a site of revolutionary type, due to its size and permanency, one of a very small number of large village sites found in the late glacial in south-west Asia (or anywhere in the world). Living together in large numbers would have confronted people with new social problems. Mobile hunter-gatherers living at low densities can cope with conflict and difficulty through dispersal: they can walk away from an argument. Several hundred people living in close dependency cannot do this. Ian Hodder sees the main thing that was domesticated in the Neolithic as not plants and animals, but society itself. Hodder feels that if there was a revolution associated with the Neolithic it was a revolution in symbolism, with house forms, stone carving, burial, pottery (when this arises) all carrying complex forms of decoration and meaning that were quite new and were aimed at helping cope with tensions between men and women. Settling down gave gender relations a new form and birth and death new values as entry into and exit from the community (we have little evidence of the former, but considerable evidence from burial). We thus suspect that the inhabitants had a complex ritual cycle, part annual and part dictated by unpredictable events like death, which we can see in the symbolism given to objects, the position of hearths, and burial.

Abu Hureyra I provided a centre of life in the form of a large village, made up of houses with their own individual centres on the hearth. From these new concentrations of people relationships spread out first to the surrounding landscape and then further afield, as indicated by the movement of seashells, obsidian, and other exotic materials. Amazing though this was, the settlement constructed after 9400 BP was quite different again. Houses were now constructed in mudbrick, with little space between them and on a layout, alignment, and form of construction that lasted for around 2,000 years. If a house was replaced every fifty years, this allows for some 400 replacements of houses in the life of the settlement. The settlement was now huge, covering some 16 hectares between 8300 and 7300 BP, housing between 5,000 and 6,000 people and requiring between 1,000 and 2,500 hectares of fields. There were now five domesticated cereals (rye, emmer, einkorn and bread wheat, two- and six-hulled barley) and lentils, peas, and vetches, with field beans and chickpeas coming in after 7300 BP. Beneath the floors of the houses were human burials, with women more numerous in burials than men. As in many sites of this age, emphasis was placed on the skull, which was often removed from the body and sometimes wrapped. Indeed, there is considerable evidence that burial was a final phase in an elaborate treatment of the body after death. Grave goods were often provided, including animal bones, bone beads, and obsidian, and such goods show no clear differences in gender. Around 7000 BP pottery was introduced, which probably caused profound changes in the way in which food was prepared and served, as well as providing a very plastic medium for symbolism, through vessel shape and painting. House walls and floors were also painted, an activity which may have occurred regularly. Figurines of clay and stone were found in the shape of animals, as are common throughout south-west Asia.

The huge mudbrick village at Abu Hureyra is one of a large number of such primary Neolithic communities found eventually from south-eastern Europe across to central Asia. Each of these shares general common elements of architecture, pots, crops, and stone tools, but each region too has its own special ways of putting together the elements. I have excavated a small early Neolithic village in present-day Turkmenistan, at the base of the Iranian plateau and on the edge of the Kara Kum desert which stretches 1,000 km to the north. Here was a small settlement of 20 to 30 houses in contemporary occupation, with beautiful painted pottery, an emphasis on einkorn as a crop, plus sheep and goat, but without any evidence of human burials. It is possible that, although the architecture of the site was permanent, the people on it were not, moving backwards and forwards between the lowland and the mountains, building and rebuilding their houses on a regular basis, so that the site built up rapidly with dates from the lowest and the highest houses indistinguishable at around 7,000 years ago. The large Turkish site of Çatal Höyük, excavated currently by Ian Hodder and his team, is enormous in size, shows many of the elements of continuity found at Abu Hureyra, but has even more marked forms of symbolism in house decorations, artefacts, and burials. People established common cultures across Europe and Asia, but used commonalities in locally specific ways, responding to the needs and aspirations that they developed through new links between people, animals, plants, and the material world.

The old view of farming stressed invention. Now issues of adoption are crucial. Any novelty has to accord with cultural norms before it will be accepted and in many cases adoption will mean that artefacts and species are changed in form or use to accord with existing practices. People, plants, and animals grew up together in various ways; not invention so much as cohabitation in a situation of changing need. Jared Diamond has estimated that there are some 148 species of herbivores and omnivores worldwide that weigh 45 kg or more. Only 14 of these species have been domesticated, leading us to wonder about the other 134 species. Even more surprising is that of the 200,000 higher plant species throughout the world; only some 100 have been domesticated and used to any extent. Despite recent massive research programmes spurred by modern agro-business, almost no extra species have been added to early rosters of food animals and plants. The vast majority of what we eat was domesticated in prehistory.

Diamond takes a functionalist view of domestication, which emphasizes food production. Zebras are nasty creatures, grizzly

Area	Domesticated		Earliest Attested Date of Domestication
	Plants	Animals	
Independent Origins of Domestication			
1. Southwest Asia	wheat, pea, olive	sheep, goat	8500 BC
2. China	rice, millet	pig, silkworm	by 7500 BC
3. Mesoamerica	corn, beans, squash	turkey	by 3500 BC
4. Andes and Amazonia	potato, manioc	llama, guinea pig	by 3500 BC
5. Eastern United States	sunflower, goosefoot	none	2500 BC
?6. Sahel	sorghum, African rice	guinea fowl	by 5000 BC
?7. Tropical West Africa	African yams, oil palm	none	by 3000 BC
?8. Ethiopia	coffee, teff	none	?
?9. New Guinea	sugar cane, banana	none	7000 BC?
Local Domestication Following Arrival of Founder Crops from Elsewhere			
10. Western Europe	poppy, oat	none	6000–3500 BC
11. Indus Valley	sesame, eggplant	humped cattle	7000 BC
12. Egypt	sycamore fig, chufa	donkey, cat	6000 BC

14. Some of the major domesticated species in each area of the world

bears too big and violent, and elephants breed too slowly, so that none of these are tractable or productive sources of food. These factors do play some part, as does the abundance of herd animals in Africa, which reduced the need to domesticate. However, relationships between people and plants and animals are partnerships and should be looked at in the round, not just on the basis of the characteristics of the non-human elements. Human marriages occasionally fail through the fault of one party, but this is pretty rare, and more generally both partners have a hand in either success or failure. Growing together over millennia has been the story of plants, animals, and humans in each continent.

Domestication is a useful term as it can catch the mutuality of this process. Domestication usually refers to the physical and behavioural alterations brought about by people in plant and animal species to make them more productive sources of food and more tractable to keep or easy to grow and process.

We have looked in detail at the Middle East; let us consider other areas more briefly. One of the debates on Africa, partly motivated by colonialist attitudes, is how far anything has been invented in Africa, or whether all elements of life have been introduced from outside. These questions partly expose a European preoccupation with origins, when it is much more important to show what use was made of things. However, recent genetic analyses of cattle and sheep indicate that in both cases there may have been domestication in eastern Africa, although in the case of cattle at least there were probably two centres of domestication, the second being somewhere in India, the source of the humped zebu cattle. The cattle complexes of eastern Africa are excellent evidence of the distinctive uses that people make of things, as cattle are not purely economic resources, although important for their milk and blood, but crucial supports to social standing and key focuses of symbolism for the Nuer, Dinka, and Masai today and for a long time in the past. Sheep have never attained the same social prominence in Africa, despite being a major herd animal in the southern parts of the continent. The horse, donkey, and camel were all domesticated in west Asia in the third millennium BC and subsequently introduced into Africa, with the water buffalo arriving as an Arab introduction a thousand years ago. Millet (both pearl and finger millet) was domesticated in eastern Africa and subsequently spread out to Asia. My favourite fruit, the banana, a staple in some areas of Africa today, has a complex history, having been domesticated in dual centres in Papua New Guinea and south-east Asia, and moved from the south-east Asian centre across the Indian Ocean to India and Africa maybe as long ago as 1500 BC.

I could continue with this roster of domestications and movements, but won't. Think of a Masai group in East Africa sitting under a tree, locally domesticated cattle in the background, eating a meal of millet and cooking bananas, washed down with a cup of tea well sweetened with sugar (a plant originating in Papua New Guinea) and consider the complexity of histories lying behind each element of the meal, only the last two of which were introduced under colonial influence. The same complexity is to be found in any part of the world, although the histories differ in time and materials. Many of the innovations associated with farming were not made for utilitarian reasons, but following the dictates of taste. The earliest forms of domestication in South America took place on the coast prior to 8000 BC and involved crops like gourds, potato, and manioc, but also tasty foods like avocados, chilli peppers, and beans. These were introduced into inland Andean sites from 4200 BC onwards, with the tasty foods moving as early as the staples and each valley choosing its own roster of crops. Food is vital for defining identity in the present and so too in the past, with each valley group making small but significant variations in their diet which marked them out as different. As Andrew Sherratt has pointed out, the earliest use of what were later staples, such as wheats, bananas, and potatoes, may have started off as luxury additions to the diet, creating variety and social differences. We cannot live by bread alone and in the early days bread may have been a special delicious addition to people's cuisine, with grains traded with some social ceremony and effect.

New elements of life were put together as they were developed locally or introduced. This was not a random process, but one which accorded with local logics of life as we can see from more recent introductions. Maori groups took readily to the *solanum* potato (first domesticated in South America some 8000 BC, as we have just seen), when it was introduced into New Zealand in the early 19th century and this was because of the existing popularity of the sweet potato (also domesticated first in South America, but moved across the Pacific at least a thousand years ago). This contrasts to the introduction of the potato into Britain by Sir Walter Raleigh (along with tobacco) which was grown for some time as an ornamental plant, as the traditions for growing, cooking, and eating such root crops were much less developed than those for dealing with cereals. Now of course no one in Britain would think of the potato as a foreign crop. New things needed to strike some chord in local ways of doing things to be accepted, even though they might later extend people's lives in unexpected ways. It is not just foodstuffs that have been accepted as innovations. The acceptance of pottery, a particularly plastic medium, created new possibilities in the creation of shape, painted effects, and other forms of surface decoration, as well as the ability of the form to echo the nature of the contents, as did the poppy-shaped pots from Europe which may have contained opium. Life combines some continuity of old ways and explorations of new possibilities.

I have saved the most contentious area for last: the possibility that each continent has its own set of myths. Myth is a controversial area in any case amongst professional archaeologists, as it taps directly into New Age and spiritual interests that easily cross the boundary between the academically respectable and the fringe. Nineteenth-century thinkers saw history as progressing through an evolutionary sequence of myth, religion, and science, with only modern Europe developing a verifiable, objective, and effective science. This attitude stills lingers in some quarters around the feeling that for archaeologists to show too much interest in myth might imply that they harbour some non-rational belief. Discussion of ritual is rife in archaeology, but this looks more at patterns of action that might be thought to have some ritual aspect and the content of beliefs is generally avoided. In the Western tradition of thought myths are seen in two ways: first, myth is opposed to reality and is fiction not fact; second, myth is opposed to rationality in a contrast going back to the ancient Greeks where *mythos* was seen as inferior to *logos* (rational thought) as a means of apprehending the world. It would seem to be waste of time to study thoughts and feelings which are both irrational and untrue, and we expect our children to grow out of a belief in the tooth-fairy or Father

Christmas. But as ever we need to be aware that the terms we use prejudice the way we approach the study of the world and the fact that for many in the world myth is a powerful force should alone make us take it a little more seriously. I will link myth and magic in the following way. Myth concerns our relationship with the world; the ubiquity of myths reflects the fact that humans are beings for whom existence is an issue. Myths outline the origins of people, animals, plants, and the world at large; they may equally speak of the end of the world, as well as what may come thereafter. Myths speak of how people ought to relate to each other and to the other powers of the cosmos, together with the perils of transgressing these relationships. Myths often use highly charged language and imagery; they are not just told, but also enacted, using artefacts to help convey vital elements, as well as dance, trance, and drugs to enhance the effect on those present.

Magic is allied to myth, but seeks to intervene in the world and change it, rather than interpret and describe it. In many places human deaths all have human causes, so that divining responsibility and bringing those responsible to justice require divination and magic. Equally, major transformations, such as smelting or casting metal, need the right sets of conditions, which include the ritual purity of the smiths and the correct spells and incantations, as well as appropriate control of fire and appropriate equipment. For those carrying it out, magic is an objective force, tapping into the productive powers of the world and not a subjective condition, just like science is for its own practitioners. To compare science and magic is not to demean science or to take an anti-science stance, but rather to set science within longer traditions of affecting the world. The big difference between science and magic is that the former pays little attention to the spiritual or moral condition of the human participants, which for the magician are vital. Stripping science of a confusing moral and cosmological dimension has improved its practical efficacy, which is unparalleled. The cost is an obvious one, excluding any questions from within the scientific process itself of whether something should be done, removing issues of morality from the scientific process.

The various continents have their own stores of myth and forms of magic. Both often concerned objects. In North America, Algonquian, Iroquian, and Siouan-speakers shared a set of religious beliefs attached to colours and the objects which manifest these colours, the most important of which were red, white/sky blue-green, and black. Red denoted contexts of anti-social action, like violence and warfare; white and sky blue-green connoted purposiveness of mind, knowledge, and the most expansive forms of being; black indicated absence of cognition and animacy. Substances with particular colours – white marine shells, porcupine quills for beadwork, rock crystals, native copper, silver or coloured stones – were linked with beings beneath the earth or water (such as the horned serpent, the panther, or the dragon) who were the guardian spirits of different medicine societies. The acquisition and use of mythically charged objects was vital to human well-being and the fertility of the natural world. Wealth was more like medicine than the European category of riches, ensuring health and well-being, and must be used wisely. By a process of 'transubstantiation', the values adhering in local objects were extended to European trade items. Europeans, in this proto-historic period, were assimilated into the network of local relationships through the significance of the trade items they brought with them: materiality was the basis for particular forms of sociality. Material coming into these northern areas originated from as far away as Mexico, indicating a shared belief system over large parts of the continent, and also parts of Siberia from which Native American populations emanate. These shared beliefs, which must have deep historical roots, include the differentiation of the realms of earth, water, and sky with some central axis joining them along which prayers travel to the spirits of each zone. Concepts of power are crucial, including that of 'medicine', which is a set of means of affecting the world in ways that are beneficial to the people concerned. The importance of visionary experience and shamans are widespread, as well as the importance of feasts and gift-giving as validations of blessings received from the spirit world. Everywhere ideas of power and of efficacy were embodied in material things, as we have seen, so that there was not the same antithesis between spirituality and materialism, as is common in Western thought.

Australian Aboriginal people also shared continent-wide forms of belief known to Europeans as the Dreaming. At the time of the creation of the world ancestral spirits moved across the surface of the earth shaping the features of each region, including the physical aspects of the landscape, such as rock formations, rivers, stands of trees, or water holes, the plants and animals (many of the ancestors were in the form of sharks, dingos, or snakes, which then became the totem or sacred animal of the group concerned) and people. Stories of the Dreaming concern not just the physics and chemistry of creating the landscape, but the creation stories contain within them indications of the correct forms of behaviour towards other species and people. Dreaming tracks run right across Australia, linking people at great removes and the tracks can be summoned up in song, painting, and dance (Bruce Chatwin's book *Songlines* provides an excellent evocation of this ritual landscape). What might appear to Europeans as purely pragmatic activity, such as hunting or gathering, requires respect for and connection to the spiritual powers of the land. The ideology of the Dreaming is of a connection to a timeless, but ever-present past and there are indications in archaeological evidence of long connections with some rock art motifs still in use today which may be 30,000 years old. Stone tools, the major source of evidence from Australia, were probably imbued with aesthetic and spiritual qualities due to colour, brilliance and the potency of their source, all challenges to the prehistorian more at home with understanding the flaking and cutting properties of stone than their cosmological significance.

Europe, Asia, and Africa have less widespread and universally shared mythologies, which is partly to do with the complexity of interconnections that existed throughout these continents and partly because of overlays of the various religions of the book, such as Buddhism, Hinduism, Islam, and Christianity. In Europe there has been considerable discussion of whether speakers of Indo-European languages shared a pantheon of gods and common religious and mythological belief. There is much room for controversy here, but let me raise the possibility that the *Iliad* and the *Odyssey*, committed to paper by someone we know as Homer, may have been the first writing of tales that were not just Greek, but of far wider Eurasian currency. If this is true then the end of prehistory with the advent of writing may provide a window into the belief systems of Iron and Bronze Age Eurasia more generally.

On each continent people have grown intimate with local plants and animals. The llama, the sweet potato, and the chilli formed the nutritional basis and the zest for people's lives in South America in a manner analogous to, but nevertheless different from, the cow, millet, and beer in Africa. The continents saw different explorations of human capacities through local involvements with the world. This is only partly because the material resources of each continent varied, but also due to the logic of magic, myth, and transformation in each region. Every continent has gone off in its own directions, with Australia and the Americas taking especially divergent paths compared to Eurasia and Africa. Separation has not precluded the movement of people, ideas, and things, but has meant that acceptance of novelty has always been predicated upon local cultural logics.

Commensualism is often a slow and continuous process, rather than a rapid and revolutionary one, which is not to say that rapid change never happens. This continuity is rooted in long-term stabilities in human populations dating back to the Pleistocene. In terms of the material world, I have focused in this chapter on plants and animals, only glancing more briefly at artefacts. In the next chapter, I shall look at material culture and start with their links to human intelligence, a term we use as a short-hand for a whole bundle of human skills and apprehensions.

Chapter 5
The nature of
human social life

A person standing on the side of a river shouts to someone on the opposite bank: 'How do you get to the other side?' The second person replies: 'You are on the other side.'

Identity depends on perspective. Definitions of identity may involve the division into two (or more) sides, or more subtle and fluid distinctions may be used. Identity is also composed of the commensual relations we have grown into with other species and with things, so that discovering the social glue in any formation is vital to social analysis. Few things are more important to us than our identity, but few are more difficult to define. Perhaps because of this importance and these difficulties, issues of identity have always been crucial to writing prehistories. Charting the coming into being of people like Us or measuring the distance to those who are foreign have always been major preoccupations. Quite who we are, or they are for that matter, is a compound of different elements of how we act towards others and towards the material world, which in turn derives from the whole nature of our social life. Identity and sociability are intimately connected with each other and with concepts of intelligence or sensibility. I shall take issues of identity as the thread to follow through the complexities of human social life, using identity in a particular sense as knowledgeable action. Let us start with a central and defining concept, that of intelligence.

The prehistory of human intelligence

Darwin was shocked. On 18 December 1832 he was rowed ashore in Good Success Bay, near the southern tip of Tierra del Fuego, to confront the 'wild men' of the area for the first time in the early stages of his life-changing voyage on the *Beagle*. His first impression was of human figures, naked despite the cold, howling and gesticulating wildly at the ship and its occupants. 'A wild man is a miserable creature', he sympathized.

> We have no reason to believe that they perform any sort of religious worship, . . . their different tribes have no government or chief, . . . the language of these people, according to our notions, scarcely deserves to be called articulate, . . . their skill in some respects may be compared to the instinct of animals, for it is not improved by experience.

The main trait of the wild man from which all these lacks stemmed was his wildness. Lacking any control over his own emotions, it was hard to exercise reason; lacking control over himself he had no ability to control the rest of the world. The fact that the inhabitants of Tierra del Fuego might have had difficult relations with passing ships before and that this might lie at the root of their reactions did not seem to have occurred to Darwin, who saw their behaviour as purely irrational. The growth of rational control over the wildness of the emotions was central to a Victorian view of the contemporary world and of human progress. The Victorian evolutionary typology, which we encountered in the last chapter, of magic, religion, and science, saw the realm of magic as animated by irrational and indeed emotional hopes for intervening in the workings of the world, misplaced hopes as compared with the procedures of science.

Intelligence is hard to define; there are as many definitions as there are people creating them. However, many definitions have core features, following a spectrum from retention of information to problem-solving to creative and innovative thought and action not carried out previously. Most definitions concern the activities of the mind and much less attention is given to the skills and capabilities of the body. You may not be surprised by now to learn that I shall emphasize the skills of the body and those so-called irrational elements of human life, such as the emotions, in attempting to chart the history of human intelligence.

I have been lucky enough to excavate at one of the most remarkable prehistoric sites in Britain – White Horse Hill at Uffington in southern Oxfordshire. The White Horse is a constructed chalk figure just below the brow of the hill at Uffington and is partly distinguished by the beauty of its form and line.

As a monument the White Horse is quite unlike most others. Ancient monuments generally survive because they are large, monumental, and resist the erosive effects of time and weather. But as a chalk figure the White Horse needs to be cared for and unless it is scoured regularly by removing the old chalk and grass and placing new white chalk on the top, the Horse will disappear into the

15. The White Horse at Uffington

background of greenery in this well-watered part of southern England. Dating the last time the sediments at the base of the Horse were exposed to sunlight has revealed the amazing fact that the Horse could be 3,000 years old. As it needs scouring every decade at least 300 such events have taken place since its construction in the late Bronze Age. Today the site is owned by the National Trust which runs outdoor courses for those suffering from the strains of urban life and it is possible to pay to go on a stress-relief course, which may involve scouring the Horse. Up until the mid-19th century scouring was carried out by the village of Uffington, when scouring was part of the May festivities which also involved rolling cheeses down the hill, horse racing, and the dangerous game of 'backswording', the object of which was to draw blood from the opponent's head with a wooden weapon. Thomas Hughes's novel *Tom Brown's School Days* carries a vivid account of one such event, and even greater detail is given in his book *The Scouring of the White Horse*. Such 19th-century events attracted many thousands of people brought in by the new railway system. Historical accounts go back to the 16th century and we can only conjecture about the nature of earlier scourings which continued despite the coming of the Romans, the Anglo-Saxons, and the Normans.

How is the White Horse in any way relevant to discussions of human intelligence? Creating the White Horse in the first place, or scouring it every decade for three millennia, does not fit in with any notion of problem-solving intelligence, but it does accord with a more general notion of care for the maintenance of social relations through the manipulation of the material world. Scouring the Horse was not a mechanical act and the significance of the Horse must have shifted as the decades and centuries rolled by: using one symbol to create and manipulate relations between people is as difficult in its own way as the creation of new symbols. Whatever the motivations of the people in the Bronze Age who constructed the Horse we can be pretty sure that stress-relief courses were not amongst them.

Aesthetic considerations, involving the impact of the material world on the senses, would have been crucial. The whiteness of the exposed chalk of the Horse against the green sward of the Downland may have been part of a broader set of symbolism. When a hillfort came to be constructed next to the Horse in the early Iron Age, the ramparts of the fort may have been faced with chalk. Visible over long distances, the fort and the Horse together would have made a powerful statement, reinforced by a linear ditch dug into the chalk for some kilometres to the south of the fort, a line of white across a green background. The manipulation of what we think of as aesthetic qualities of the world is vital to creating human relations which have particular values attached, using 'value' in its broadest sense. In the case of the Horse, hillfort, and linear ditch we cannot be sure what these values were, but some mix of possession of both the landscape and the powers emanating from the land would have been crucial to the appreciation of the figure of the Horse. How the colours and qualities of the landscape were reflected in clothing, houses, and artefacts we can only speculate, but people of later prehistory in this part of Britain would have lived in a rich aesthetic world encompassing pottery, metalwork, woodwork, and textiles, as well as song, story, and dance – the making and exchange of which would have helped attach values to their human relationships at a local domestic level and further afield. Indeed, by later prehistory, materials entered Britain in the form of amber from the Baltic, coral from the Mediterranean or Red Sea, and metals from many parts of Western and Central Europe. People's horizons were broad and the standing of an individual or a group depended on their ability to cultivate and manipulate relationships with others throughout Britain and Europe and having the right sense of style to deploy the bronzes, gold, and amber in the most telling sorts of social theatre. The manipulation of pottery, metal or textiles to form social relations drew on ways of shaping the world going back to the Neolithic and beyond. The Victorian gatherings on White Horse Hill stood at the end of a long tradition of large public social events in that place, with ever-changing meanings to be sure, but with a complex set of motives of pleasing the powers of the universe and raising the profile of the group.

Human intelligence as a creative combination of the human and the material goes back to a key argument of mine advanced in Chapter 3: we are the only animal species which makes its social life through shaping the material world. The scouring of the Horse is an act that requires little technical knowledge (even I have done it!), but needs a deep appreciation of its continuing social consequences. Human intelligence exists across a spectrum ranging from technically sophisticated acts to socially creative ones and may mix the social and the material in different combinations. The anthropologist Alfred Gell coined the term 'the technology of enchantment' to highlight processes of making or artefacts resulting from these processes which moved people to wonder and to awe. The power of the object to elicit emotions like wonder reinforced the power of the maker, as one who had the technical knowledge and right cosmological standing to distil something of the wonder of the world into things. The Horse is an enchanting object, leading us to wonder and to speculation in the present, as in the past, and in this sense the power of the original makers endures, even if their original intentions do not.

So here I will disagree with Darwin – people of the past were not wild in the sense that they were governed by uncontrolled emotions due to the lack of a developed faculty of reason. Emotions can be powerful, occasionally overwhelming us; but so too can thought. Just as thought is not predictable, linear, or controlled, nor are emotions random, unpredictable, or uncontrolled. We can be suddenly struck by a thought or we can cultivate an emotion. But for many Victorians human history was the story of the growing control of reason over the emotions, a view surviving in less well articulated form today. What if we cannot clearly separate thought and feeling? A state of inspiration is a powerful intellectual and emotional experience deriving from a new feel for the world and novel possibilities of shaping the world in words and objects. For the most part we have a highly structured and predictable emotional life; powerful emotions arise either through unforeseen events or being deliberately stirred up through ritual action. Indeed, ritual and the unforeseen are linked, as many rituals are designed to cope with the irruption of death into the world of the living, to transmit the joy of birth, or mark rites of passage.

Transformations are central to a notion of intelligence which focuses on the joint manipulation of the material and social worlds. And transformations are dangerous processes hemmed around with magic and ritual. Western views of cause and effect have come to separate sets of physical processes known through biology, physics, and chemistry from the social relations making up the human world. The production of metalwork requires an understanding of pyrotechnology, the chemistry of ores and compounds, and the right sequence of actions and combination of materials needed to produce bronze or steel. Westerners see the people involved in production as technicians, more or less skilled and experienced in understanding physical processes, able to do the right thing at the correct time. Their religious beliefs or degree of sexual abstinence could have no effect on the outcome of their production. For many African smiths metal production is part of larger processes of production and transformation, linked as much to the conception and birth of children as it is to other forms of material production, such as the firing of pots. Many African conceptions of the world link human fertility, the growing and processing of food, and craft production in cycles of transformation in which the human and spirit worlds collaborate to ensure human well-being. Westerners tend to make a distinction between technology, derived from an empirical understanding of physical cause and effect, and magic, which is essentially meaningless hocus-pocus, whose only possible importance could be a psychological one to convince the smiths that things are going well. For many African smiths, smelting is a process similar to a woman giving birth and many furnaces are embellished with female symbols, the male smiths acting as the fathers, with actual women rigorously excluded from the process and sex between the male smiths and women prohibited while iron working is taking place. It is often thought that sexual intercourse generates heat, so that the woman's blood and male semen are heated to produce the child. The application of heat during cooking is also vital to human life. The heat generated by iron working is extreme and threatening. Iron can be made into weapons and used violently, making it a dangerous substance, so that any hint of discord amongst the smiths will cause their work to fail, as will a drop of blood shed in the foundry, even if this occurred through harmless accident. No distinction is made between technical expertise and ritual knowledge, between science and magic; smiths must have a mastery of all aspects of their craft, however Westerners might categorize these, making them either powerful and influential people in other areas of their lives or dangerous outcasts.

We know from ethnographies of the 19th and 20th centuries something of the skills and knowledge of recent smiths and the symbolism with which their workshops and tools were imbued and we can follow some of the same symbolism back into the prehistoric past where words fail us and, indeed, the widespread nature of the beliefs surrounding iron production in sub-Saharan Africa indicate their antiquity. Furnaces are known from prehistoric periods in western and southern Africa which have breasts and female genitalia and in some areas similar decorations are found on cooking pots, which also bear the application of heat in the process of transformation. What modern Western thought has characterized as technological or economic developments ushering in the start of the Iron Age would have been conceived differently by those involved in developing iron working in Africa at least 1,500 years ago and would have represented new sets of possibility in creating novel sets of human relationships and extending ideas concerning the transformations of which the world was capable. It is not a question of judging whether the Western or African conceptions of the making of metal are more correct and so judging between science and magic; both have their efficacies. However, I would argue that, in one area, African conceptions are more realistic. If human beings are the only species to create their social relations through manipulating the material world, then emphasizing the joint making of people and of things does justice to the linked nature of physical processes and human social life, so that the making of children and the making of metal may have subtle links. Intelligence is deployed in thinking about how physical and social relations are transformed together, which involves an understanding of physical processes and social ones. Western science shines a laser beam on physical processes, but has lost a sense of magic concerning how the world and people work together. Understanding prehistory may help us recapture some of that magic.

Transformations are manifest in connections, not only between people and things, but also between various sorts of artefacts which are aesthetic in nature. In Europe prehistoric bronzes were probably given shiny surfaces to evoke images of silver and gold, effects hard to recreate and appreciate after up to 4,000 years of burial. Bronze to gold formed a spectrum of precious metal objects, a spectrum which was extended when bronze vessel shapes were echoed in pottery. In China green was encouraged as a surface colour for bronze, due to the importance of jade, the use of which went back to the Neolithic and beyond. Painted Samarran-period pots made in Mesopotamia around 6500 BC had decorations that imitated the weave of baskets, which predated the pottery; the caulking of baskets with clay may have helped give rise to pottery making. In the late Neolithic of Scandinavia, delicately flaked flint daggers imitated the copper daggers that had come into vogue further south on the north German plain and in Central Europe.

In the western Pacific, from Papua New Guinea to Samoa, Lapita pottery found from 1500 BC carried complex toothed decorations

16. A Scandinavian late Neolithic flint dagger

that may have echoed tattoos made by toothed implements on human skin. A tattooed person carrying a pot formed part of a complex field of decoration, part clay, part skin. In many parts of the world people and animals have been buried together and treated in a similar fashion, indicating that being animal and being human may have had significant overlaps. Objects, people, and animals may have borne sets of associations that extended across more than one class of artefact as we would define it, opening up a wide range of metaphorical associations testing human aesthetic senses and skills. Again we have varied aesthetics, with their own continental histories.

Human beings learn to make infinite numbers of discriminations about the world – just close your eyes and feel your clothing to register how many textures of fabric you can distinguish. The same is true of any other sense. How many meals do you know by smell? Can you distinguish all the members of your household from the sound of their feet on the stairs? How many shades of blue can you see? These discriminations I would call aesthetics, albeit aesthetics of an everyday kind. They are values we attach to the world so that we can live in a particular manner within it. Values need learning through an education of the senses. The reciprocal of these aesthetic qualities of the world is the range of human responses they evoke. There are emotions attached to our perceptions – a particular set of feet on the stairs may fill us with relief or dread, blue may have connotations of wonder or holiness, a smell may set off a wave of disgust. The English word 'feeling' usefully captures some of the link between our sensory appreciations of the world and emotions – what something feels like physically may be linked to what we feel about a state of affairs. Feelings can be hurt or dampened to the point where we don't feel anything. And feelings can be indefinite, exploratory, intuitive, such as when we say 'Something just didn't feel right' about a particular person or situation. Feelings are a part of our intelligent appreciation of the world, although they are rather different from rational thought and they provide us with a blend of the physical and the emotional which is vital for us to use in navigating through the world.

Being intelligent is not purely to do with mental operations of the human brain, but involves all our senses of sight, touch, smell, taste, and hearing, singly or in combination. Our senses need cultivating through being directed in particular ways, to appreciate the varying greenness of bronze or the heft of a copper dagger. Synaesthesia is a condition in which the inputs of the senses get mixed up. For those suffering from this condition shapes can have a taste and sounds colours, creating a cross-cutting sensorium which is both confusing and creative. Some cultures have cultivated a multi-sensorial approach to the world, replete with analogical reasoning, and notable among these are the cultures of Central America. Copper, gold, and silver were the only metals known in Central America (Mexico and the countries immediately to the south) in pre-Columbian times and none of these held a good cutting edge, so that other substances were sought. A main provider of cutting tools was the volcanic glass, obsidian, which was widely used and traded elsewhere in the world, including the western Pacific, from 20,000 years ago onwards, the Middle East from at least 10,000 years ago, and East Africa for many thousands of years. Obsidian is a form of glass, being as sharp as any other form and is still used today in delicate eye operations. One of the great advantages of obsidian for the prehistorian is that many sources are chemically distinct, allowing the possibility that obsidian tools can be traced back to their origins, allowing patterns of trade to be reconstructed over long periods of time. Much effort has gone into sourcing obsidian in Central America for sites dating to the last 3,000 years and into understanding changing methods of working obsidian. Obsidian has mainly been understood in economic terms (I shall return to economics below), but other elements of significance need to be brought into any account. Two aspects of obsidian can be highlighted. First, it is associated with volcanoes and so with the underworld, a link strengthened by the fact that, from later prehistory onwards, it was mined. Temples were frequently located near volcanoes, close to the destructive powers of the earth, and the links between sacredness, creation, and destruction helped explain obsidian's power to forge social relationships. From late prehistory at least obsidian knives were instruments of death and sacrifice, able to dispatch a victim and remove their heart. The Aztecs used obsidian mirrors as magical forms of divination, as a means to get in touch with the gods, a use that predates them and also survives into the colonial period.

The dark power of obsidian only partly derived from its uncommon sharpness, which was reinforced by links with the creative and destructive powers of the universe. It was also metaphorically placed in relationship to jade, the property of rulers, which could bring greenness and fertility to a local area, and turquoise, connected to the gods and which could emit smoke, like clouds against a blue sky. A Western notion of economy works with a scale of values created by usefulness, human labour power, or rarity. Obsidian was useful, especially if you wanted to offer a human heart to the gods, but its value derived from more mysterious sets of associations than those of utility, giving it ambiguous, but powerful qualities through which to affect human relations many miles from its source. Material things are not appreciated through one sense, but a number, giving us a synaesthetic reaction to the world, as sensory inputs mix and mingle. We can feel the sharpness of an obsidian blade on our skin, see its colour to the eye, hear the ringing tone of a blade, and its weight in the hand, all of which combine into our feel for the substance and its potentials.

Like science, the notion of economics divides people and objects, or rather only allows them to meet in particular ways, around the satisfaction of human needs. An emphasis on physical wants may allow us to understand later human history as more basic human needs come to the fore as motivations, due to population growth and scarcity imposed on some people by the rest. However, in earlier periods when people were fewer and power structures less impoverishing for those lowest on the social pyramid, it was relatively easy to provide food and shelter and to meet everyone's calorific requirements. Values other than those of need and utility flourished, allowing complex and tangled links between objects and objects, and objects and people. The scope for a purely economic analysis shrinks in prehistory, when the significance of broader human values blossomed before becoming subject to the weight of brute necessity. Many of the tools of analysis honed through work on the modern world, like the methods of economics, prove blunt instruments when applied to the values of prehistory.

Gender and sexuality

The aesthetic values arising from the sensory qualities of objects influence the manner in which people act as social beings. We have looked briefly at the values attached to things; now let us turn to the values linked to bodies. A major element of all human societies is the distinction between genders, although to say that all people make gender distinctions is not say that all people make the same distinctions. A commonplace of recent gender analysis is to see gender as the cultural use that people make of the biological distinctions of sex. Physical differences between men and women of genitalia, body size, and shape are part of the raw materials for creating gender, but not the end of the story. Many groups distinguish more than two genders (the *hijras* of India or the Two Spirits of Native American groups are both well-known examples of people who are neither men or women) and for some people gender is not fixed, but derives from the situation in which individuals are placed. For instance, in Papua New Guinea penises can give birth in certain instances, making them a temporarily female organ, rather than a purely male one, and blood drawn from the penis in initiation rites is seen as analogous to menstrual blood, with its connotations for men of the power of fertility and the danger of female pollution.

Knapp and Meskell have examined a series of physical representations of the human figure from Cyprus in the Chalcolithic (Copper Age) and Bronze Age.

They feel that these figurines provide a commentary on what it means to be an individual in these periods, looking at the tendency to experience oneself as a distinct entity, how this sense of self may vary as experienced through age, status, sex, or ethnicity, and how this results in the cultural experience of being a man or a woman in a particular time or place. Other researchers have classified the human figures in terms of being either male or female, although some have both a penis and a vulva. They also question the

17. Red polished ware double-headed plank figurine from Dhenia, Cyprus, showing individual facemarks and jewellery

distinction that has been made between the Chalcolithic stone pendants and the Bronze Age plank figures, mainly made in clay. Inevitably some people have seen these figures as mother goddesses, but Knapp and Meskell see many of the figures as trying to harmonize the sexual characteristics of men and women, rather than emphasizing differences. Through the Bronze Age there is a growing emphasis on figures with individual adornment and jewellery, as well as face decorations that might be interpreted as masks, tattoos, or face-painting. There were larger numbers of individual burials in the Bronze Age compared with the communal burials of earlier periods. The greater rise in the definition of the individual occurs against a background of increased numbers and sizes of settlements, the refinement of craft technologies, and intensified agricultural production, connected with the development of elites. Knapp and Meskell stress that individuality should not be seen in the same terms as modern individualism and rather than seeing people as parcelled up into fixed divisions of gender, age, and rank, we should understand this as a time of social fluidity when gender and other elements of identity existed as a spectrum, from which people could choose to develop various aspects of their personality, possibly reviewing and changing this choice at various times in their lives. The imprint of the material world on the human body, through jewellery, clothing, cosmetics, or tattoos, is vital in creating socially salient categories, which may derive power from being flexible and strategic, not fixed and rigid.

Gender is something to be created and performed, rather than inherited as an accident of biology and an unchanging dimension of biography. The creation of gendered identity can be a complex business and needs a series of material supports. The so-called Venus figurines of the Upper Palaeolithic period in Europe are distributed widely from the present-day Ukraine to France. These well-modelled clay or stone figurines have been seen as mother goddesses, connected with the fertility of people and the cultural landscape generally. More recently it has been argued that the figurines represent the whole life cycle of a reproductive woman, including pre-menstrual and post-menopausal states, and that they might have been used for women-only forms of education and initiation to teach girls about the female body. Figurines may have been made and used by women in secret, implying that there was some separation between men and women. Alternatively, as happens in many parts of the contemporary world, the figurines may have been used in the initiation of boys, where metaphors of female fertility and pregnancy are important as education about general social reproduction. In this case, maleness may have been constructed through reference to women's bodies, implying a more complementary notion of gender and possibly sexuality than is evoked by the image of secret female rites. Whatever was the case with Upper Palaeolithic gender relations (and it is obviously difficult to pin this down), it appears that roles and relations were enacted through material forms, such as figurines, and not read straight from the biology of the body.

One Venus figurine comes from the site Dolní Vestonice in the present-day Czech Republic. This was a huge open site from the height of the last Ice Age which contained evidence of many habitation structures and burials. The burial which concerns us here was of three bodies lying side by side in a shallow pit.

The two outer bodies appear anatomically male and the inner one was of indeterminate sex, but might have been female. They were laid on their backs and then had branches placed over them which were burnt. Bits of clothing or body decoration survive in the form of pierced seashells, and wolf and Arctic fox teeth. The bodies were liberally sprinkled with red ochre, especially round their heads. The central figure had a block of ochre between her/his thighs and the left-hand figure is extending his hands into this pubic area of the central person. He had a stake driven through his pelvic area into the coccyx and although he appears to be looking at the central figure s/he has turned away, directing her gaze at the person to her left. Physical anthropological analysis has revealed that the central person had a congenital hip condition, *coxa vara*, which would have caused them to walk with a slight limp. It is tempting to see this person as central in all senses, someone whose physical characteristics helped mark them out, ambiguity and difference lending power to their statements and actions. Quite what the symbolism contained in the burial was we shall never know. It may have been celebration, punishment for sexual transgressions (a

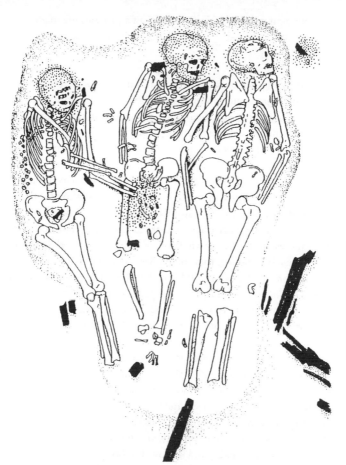

18. The triple burial from Dolní Věstonice

favourite with popular interpretations – some sort of love-triangle
of the type the tabloids constantly seek to expose), or due to
untimely death. The pubic regions of two figures do seem to
have been picked out, leading us to think of sex, and the presence
of so much red ochre may have had links to blood, menstrual
or otherwise. As Nancy Banks-Smith, the *Guardian* TV

correspondent wisely said in the review of a programme made partly about this burial: 'They were buried in code and we have lost the key.'

The Dolní Vestonice burial combines intimations of sex and ambiguity of gender, emphasizing that these two dimensions of life are vital to the values attached to human actions in many times and places. Sex and gender are points at which the physical nature of our bodies and their social impacts meet, mixing what we tend to separate as the biology of the body on the one hand and the realm of cultural action on the other. Nature and culture are too complicated to be separated in this way; neither forms the foundation for the other. The burials at Dolní Vestonice indicate a powerful set of experiences for the individuals concerned and the community as a whole and we do not know what sort of social theatre led up to the triple burial, but the fact that the bodies seem to have been buried after *rigor mortis* had worn off hints that the whole process was not quick. The sheer physicality of the experience was vital to its impact: the incipient decay of the bodies as they were dressed in their burial best, acting out in silent mime roles important to those still living; the sprinkling of ochre, which may have mixed with real blood; the driving of a wooden stake into one body and the sudden roar of the flames at the end of the burial would have helped to heighten the already taut emotions of sisters, brothers, or parents of the trio and we can only guess what these emotions might have been – joy, fear, disgust, relief – or all of these together, experienced by various members of the community. Our bodies are the sites of pleasure, happiness, pain, and sorrow. But bodies are not purely private theatres of sensation. They are linked to the bodies of others, most intimately through sex or physical care, and indirectly through the education of the senses and emotions. Sensual experience is used socially, in initiation rites which often involve pain, or forms of performance like dance. Sex and gender are aspects of bodily being and actions vital to our identities. The past codes of these identities are hard for the prehistorian to crack, but so central are these issues that considerable effort is worthwhile.

Explorations

An intelligent approach to the world is partly displayed through the encounter with novelty, or the creation of novelty. Explorations and settlement of new parts of the world extend people's social and physical knowledge, creating new sets of skills in the process. As we have seen, modern humans have colonized the whole of the earth's surface over the last 40,000 years, with the partial exception of Antarctica. The last major portion of the world to be settled was not a continent, but the Pacific Ocean. Extension of human life into the Pacific created new ways of being in the world with their own sets of physical skills and sensitivities to the physical and human worlds. Europeans consider the ability to sail and navigate at sea to be the result of a series of technological inventions and innovations, the concrete outcomes of problem-solving intelligence – the ability to know one's latitude is a tale of timepieces, astronomical observations, and charts. How was it that the biggest of all oceans, the Pacific, was crossed, starting some 3,500 years ago and completed with the settlement of Hawai'i, Easter Island, and New Zealand, less than a millennium ago? The necessary skills and abilities have a long prehistory.

In 1985 I was digging a site called Matenkupkum, a large, dry cave on the east coast of a place called New Ireland, one of the larger offshore islands of Papua New Guinea. The cave is metres from where the Pacific Ocean crashes onto the reef, and whilst digging I could look out of the cave aware that, directly ahead of me, but behind the horizon, were thousands of kilometres of open sea. The next landfalls are the tiny islands of Kiribati (formerly the Gilbert and Ellice Islands), easy enough to miss and then nothing but sea to the western seaboard of North America. Matenkupkum is a large, open cave in the coral limestone on a terrace above the present-day beach. Its name translates as the 'cave of the swifts' due to the birds that nest in fissures in the roof of the cave, one point on their long-distance travels across the globe. Matenkupkum had a stalactite

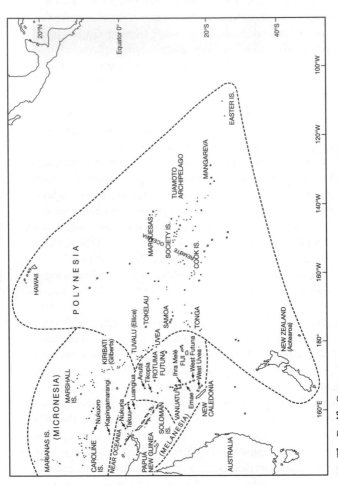

19. The Pacific Ocean

20. The cave of Matenkupkum, New Ireland, Papua New Guinea, during excavation

pillar in its centre said to contain the spirit of a woman, who could be seen down on the reef at nights of the full moon, but she was a benign spirit and the cave was not seen locally as a place of danger. What I wondered about as the dig progressed was how the finds from the cave fitted into the story of the human colonization of the Pacific, and how people had originally crossed those huge expanses of ocean?

The cave held intriguing finds. One set of these was from quite a different story to that of the colonization of the Pacific. Across the front of the cave a trench had been dug by Japanese soldiers in the Second World War, when Matenkupkum was one of a number of armed positions along the coast to protect a telephone line that ran from one centre of operations to another. This was a poignant sort of archaeology as we removed saucepans, boots, bullets and saké bottles from the trench. A local man sang me a song in Japanese he had been taught at that time, which he said concerned the demise of America. He looked embarrassed, uncertain how I would react. I wasn't sure what I felt. It was an ambiguous moment for both of us.

The rest of our finds were very different. In the upper levels of the cave earths large coral limestone slabs had been laid as the foundation for a hearth, much as people do today. Local people digging with me speculated excitedly as to who of their ancestors was responsible for this hearth and why they had no stories concerning such a thing. Connected with the hearth were large numbers of bones of wallaby, cuscus (a tree-dwelling marsupial), rats of a nicely edible size, thousands of shells from the reef, together with the bones of reef and deep-sea fish and numbers of rather crude stone tools, including small flakes of obsidian. Much of the deposit we dug out was ash from the hearth. Here was evidence of a camp, where people hunted animals on the grasslands and rainforest behind the cave, but mainly gathered shellfish and fish from the reef below. The obsidian, we were pretty sure even while excavating it, came from the volcanoes of adjacent New Britain some 350 kilometres away. Here was a hint of longer distance connections in a mass of material otherwise obviously local. About a metre below the layers of the hearth was a deposit of a different type. Local stone tools were still there, as were fish and shellfish, but the only land animals were the bones of snakes and lizards and there was no obsidian. Material was much less abundant, without any evidence of hearths or burning.

Eating fish and dried biscuits at lunch time, I would sit and look out over the ocean and run through the finds in my mind. There was no pottery in the cave at all, which either indicated that it was used prior to the introduction of pottery into this part of New Guinea a little over 3,000 years ago, or that no pots had ended up in the cave (which seemed unlikely). We did not know when obsidian or hearths were first used, but a few thousand years ago seemed reasonable. The bottom-most layers looked to result from quite a different form of occupation, but the shells down the bottom still had their original colour, which seemed to contradict other indications that these lower deposits might be ancient. Prehistorians are worried about the age of things and, working in unknown archaeological territory, the age of the finds from Matenkupkum were my initial means of comparing them to finds from other known sites and thus making sense of them. As I was to find there were no directly comparable finds to help me make sense of this site.

Let us cut to a scene a year later at a conference at the Australian Museum in Sydney where the results of the expedition as a whole were being presented. The excavations at Matenkupkum had been part of a broader project in which 14 different teams had excavated throughout the offshore islands of Papua New Guinea, organized by Jim Allen and myself. It is still the hardest thing I have ever done. The Sydney conference was the initial culmination of a lot of work; excitement was high. We had heard that morning about the first find of a bronze from within New Guinea, imported from south-east Asia; a wonderful set of Lapita period sites, some 3,300 years old, where water-logged conditions had preserved the remains of houses built over the shallow waters of the reef, together with plant remains, shell tools, and obsidian, intermingled with spectacular Lapita pottery with the most intricate toothed designs. A seasoned archaeologist, not given to hyperbole, said that he felt the hairs on the back of his neck stand up when he saw the reconstructions of some of the pots, so powerfully did they evoke past skills and sensibilities. We had also heard about three other cave sites in New Ireland, two of which had deposits dating to 15,000 BP and another which was hard to date. The fourth cave was Matenkupkum. A female student is presenting the results from the excavation, which she is working on for her thesis. I know she is nervous, as this is her first big conference paper, the audience is a distinguished and potentially critical one, and the results are controversial, but she carries it off well. I had been uncertain as to whether to present the work myself, but Nola had done so much good work it was a shame to deny her the chance to present it; on the other hand I didn't want to expose her to a sceptical audience.

Scepticism might have been aroused by the dates from Matenkupkum, which showed that those basal levels were 35,000 years old. People must have sailed into New Ireland, which was always an island even at periods of lowest sea level, making this possibly the oldest evidence of island colonization in the world. The islands of the Mediterranean and the Caribbean, the two other great sets of islands, were only permanently occupied around 6000 BC, although visited before this. Similarly, the fish bones and shells were evidence of some of the oldest marine fishing and shellfish gathering in the world. Not that age was everything, but here was evidence of an unusually precocious set of maritime traditions, which provided a long backdrop to the large-scale, but recent, open-ocean colonization. The uniqueness of the Pacific island evidence was soon reinforced when we learnt that the northern tip of the Solomon Islands had been occupied almost 30,000 years ago, which involved a journey over the horizon, overcoming a considerable psychological barrier.

Skills of voyaging and navigation are only part of what was needed for successful island colonization. The basal levels at Matenkupkum show how long ago these were developed. The upper levels from the site, dating to between 21,000 and 10,000 years ago, contained a different part of the story. Islands generally have fewer plants and animals than larger landmasses, and foodstuffs can be scarce, so that getting to islands can be difficult, but staying alive once there can be even harder. It is notable that both the Mediterranean and Caribbean islands were only permanently settled once the intensive forms of land-use associated with farming were developed, allowing people to extract much food from a relatively small land area. The earliest inhabitants of Matenkupkum were certainly not farmers and the bones from these lowest layers indicate a small number of lizards, snakes, and birds as the only terrestrial foods. People seem to have overcome these constraints by moving themselves between scarce resources, living a mobile lifestyle in which the sea was vital as a source of food and of movement. After 21,000 years ago things changed and we started to find the bones of the grey cuscus, an arboreal marsupial, and evidence of obsidian from neighbouring New Britain. We know that the obsidian was imported, as no sources exist on New Ireland, but it seems too that the grey cuscus was also an import, soon to be joined by a new wallaby species, both ultimately originating from mainland New Guinea.

Such imports represent a new strategy. Instead of moving people between resources, resources were now moved to people. These were groups thought to be hunter-gatherers, yet they were certainly not passively suffering the constraints of their environment, but actively overcoming it, through moving around wild animals (and possibly plants) together with important materials such as obsidian. Pacific prehistorians talk of transported landscapes in relation to the smaller islands of the remote Pacific, all settled in the last 3,500 years. When sailing to Tonga, Tahiti, or Easter Island, colonists loaded their canoes with root crops like taro and yams, trees such as breadfruit and bananas, and the pig, dog, and chicken. The first few centuries after landfall saw considerable replacement of the natural plants, the extinction of indigenous birds (the moa of New Zealand being the best known case), and their replacement with introduced plants and animals, often planted and used in ways that mimicked the original flora and fauna, giving some protection to these fragile ecosystems. What Europeans took to be natural paradises in places like Tahiti or Samoa were some of the most carefully managed landscapes on earth.

The origins of these transported landscapes can be traced back to the evidence from Matenkupkum some 21,000 years ago, as can the evidence for seafaring and fishing which goes back 35,000 years. The ability to move freely by sea and to cope with relatively restricted sets of resources on islands laid the basis for island life not found anywhere else in the world, showing that there were quite separate traditions of life developed in various parts of the globe.

Prehistory ended in Hawai'i on 17 January 1779. On this day Captain James Cook came ashore at Kealakekua Bay to a most rapturous reception; an estimated 10,000 people were there to greet him. He and his crew had been engaged in a fruitless search along the Canadian west coast for the north-west passage, which it was thought might provide a speedy route between the Pacific and the Atlantic, a hope we now know to be misplaced. As winter came on in these northern climes, Cook sailed south to overwinter in Tahiti, a place he knew well from his first two voyages. Unexpectedly, on their way south, they encountered Hawai'i, being the first Europeans to do so and roughly a thousand years later than the initial Polynesian colonists of these islands. Having mapped part of the big island of Hawai'i and taken part in some dramatic encounters with the locals, Cook left Kealakekua Bay to resume the journey to Tahiti on 4 February 1779, saying to the Hawaiians that he would be back next year. All would have been well had not the foremast sprung on the *Resolution* a few days out from Hawai'i. Coming back to Kealakekua Bay to get a replacement mast, Cook and his crew were met with a totally different reception. Thefts and confrontations escalated, culminating in the taking of a cutter on the night of 13 February. The next morning, Cook and a party of marines went ashore to take Kalaniopu'u, the paramount chief, hostage against the return of the boat. Returning to the shore with the chief, Cook and his men were surrounded by angry warriors. Cook fired his gun at a man about to strike him but the shot could not penetrate the warrior's protective matting. Seeing this the Hawaiian warriors ran forward, killing Cook and four marines, probably using iron daggers made in Birmingham and traded by his crew to the Hawaiian nobles. His men in offshore boats watched aghast as the great explorer died, his body carried off in triumph.

In order to understand Cook's death we need to consider the Hawaiian point of view. When Cook and his crew arrived, the Hawaiians were engaged in an annual festival, four months in length, during which processions took place in a clockwise direction around each of the Hawaiian islands with the god Lono at their head. Lono was the priests' and people's god and the Makahiki represented a period during which the normal social order was overturned. During this time the chiefs went into hiding and their god Ku with them. At the end of each Makahiki there was a ritual confrontation between Lono and Ku through which Lono was driven off, not to return again for another eight months until the start of the next Makahiki. This confrontation restored the rule of the chiefs. The social year was intimately tied to the agricultural round. With Ku restored, planting began, utilizing the February rains, one such rainstorm bringing about the damage to the *Resolution's* mast. Harvest took place at the beginning of the Makahiki festival. The calendar was also a basic part of the transported landscapes Hawaiians brought with them across the Pacific, specifying how plants and animals should be used, together with the human and cosmological implications of each part of the year. This ritual calendar provides the framework for Cook's death.

The anthropologist, Marshall Sahlins, has argued that Hawaiians, trying to make sense of the first encounter with Europeans, took Cook to be the commoners' god Lono. Cook arrived when the Makahiki was under way and in mapping Hawai'i his ships followed the clockwise progress of the Lono procession around the island. Cook came ashore on 17 January, just at the end of the procession and acquiesced in a number of rituals in which he was dressed as Lono, then unknowingly underwent a ritual confrontation with Kalaniopu'u. His departure for Tahiti was slightly late for the Hawaiians, but his promise to return next year was reassuring as it confirmed Cook/Lono's role in the ritual cycle. The big problem was his unprecedented return a few days later, which to the Europeans was caused by unforeseen and unwanted practical events, but to the Hawaiians looked like Lono challenging the power of the chiefs and with it the whole cosmological and social order, a challenge confirmed when Cook took Kalaniopu'u hostage. To use Sahlins's joke – this was one time when God was indeed an Englishman.

Cook's death resulted from the meeting of two social logics, which were each internally consistent, but based on different premises. Hawaiian logic was part of their ancient Pacific heritage, brought by the first colonists to those islands and shared with all other Polynesian groups, but given special expression in Hawai'i. The prehistory of Hawai'i is one of the creation of a sacred landscape, with temples, habitation sites, field systems, and fish ponds developing over a millennium and achieving modern expression in the four centuries before Cook's coming. The ritual system regulated not just the landscape, but also human relations. Wakea (sky-father) and Papa (earth-mother) are parents of the islands of Hawai'i and of human offspring, setting the basis for the taboo system, where women were seen as defiling in contrast to the sacredness of men. The two genders must not eat together, and women were forbidden to eat certain foods, such as pig, coconut, and bananas, which have male symbolic connotations. A further separation of rank also ran through the landscape, ensuring that commoners (*maka'ainana*) and chiefs (*ali'i*) maintained a proper distance between each other. The basis of this distance was cosmological: the chiefs were closer to the gods than were the commoners and more able to influence divine powers. Hawaiian history was constructed so as to link philosophy and action into general precepts used as guides for living well.

In many ways, Hawaiian suspicions that Cook had come to overturn the accepted order turned out to be well-founded. In 1812 the taboo system was given up and Christianity adopted, which simultaneously reordered relations between men and women, chiefs and commoners, and all human beings to cosmological powers. Today identity for Native Hawaiians is a complex compound of past Polynesian inheritances, ultimately traceable to the offshore islands of New Guinea 35,000 years ago, their history since 1779, and contemporary life in a multicultural state of the US, where land they feel to be theirs is owned and used by people of European, Japanese, and Chinese descent. The past is deployed in the service of the politics of the present, where Polynesian inheritance is stressed but common cause is also made with Native American organizations on the US mainland, who are also attempting to overcome genocide and dispossession.

Colonial and post-colonial identities result from a clash of mythologies. Cook is seen as the great explorer and harbinger of capitalism (Adam Smith's global agent, as he has been described), using and developing new forms of navigation to travel and chart a major portion of the earth's surface, together with gathering systematic information on the peoples of the Pacific. Such rational control over the world expressed in charts and maps met the cyclical conceptions of Polynesians where the differences between the sacred and profane were blurred, so that a person could be a god. Europeans celebrated a new-found ability to navigate huge expanses of ocean without really reflecting on the ability of the so-called primitive peoples they encountered to do the same through a feel for wind and tide, close observation of the stars, and long knowledge of Pacific seaways, transmitted through story, song, and actual voyages.

Our identities are not fixed, but exploratory. In different continents people have experimented with how to transform the world, so as to transform themselves. As with the Hawaiian year or African iron working, cycles of transformations are well known and understood. Other events are unexpected, putting normal common sense at risk. The coming of Cook for the Hawaiians was an extreme event, but war, sudden death, and natural disaster all have to be coped with. Explorations of the world are simultaneously explorations of the human body and being, charting the range of sensory experiences possible in the world and the values that can be attached to such experiences. Writing prehistory is a recapitulation of past experiences, re-exploring the creative possibilities of bodies and materials and their varied cultural logics.

All our identities and histories are partly mythologically based, resting on unexamined principles and taken-for-granted assumptions. The further we go back in time the more our myths flourish, unconstrained by direct knowledge. Socrates' dictum that the unexamined life is not worth living lies at the heart of much critical Western thought, encouraging the power of *logos* over *mythos*. The Victorians celebrated their own logic, but loved other peoples' myths. In this we are their children. Such attitudes have acted to dam up a rich reservoir of myth in our culture, making it an object of study rather than belief. Prehistory is a rare area where myth comes to life and this is a major part of its attraction. This is not to say that we are making up prehistory, or that we should do so. Ultimately the past is of interest for present purposes; it means nothing in itself. To give the past maximum power in the present we should celebrate and enhance its mythological properties, but ensure that the myths we are working through are healthy ones by which to live. The careful empirical examination of the past is not at odds with our use of prehistory to understand present relations between men, women, and children, between those of different cultures, and between those with a deep belief in the divine on those who have lost such beliefs. For Cook to understand Hawaiian motives on the day of his death would have required a heroic effort of sympathetic understanding and the same was true of Kalaniopu'u. But a successful effort on everyone's part to understand foreign social logics would have changed the history that unfolded on 14 February 1779 and might subsequently have changed a clash of cultures into something approaching sympathetic understanding. These are utopian hopes to be sure, but more necessary now than at any time in the recent past.

Prehistory puzzles 3

A vital, but controversial, element of life in many areas of the world, although maybe especially in Britain, is that of class. Many would see class divisions as a major issue in most Western societies. Although class is something that is acknowledged at an anecdotal level, it is notoriously difficult to define. Income is a rather confusing measure, as there is quite a lot of overlap between working class, middle class, and aristocratic wealth. Class is partly about attitudes, but attitudes are very hard to pin down and define. A student working on kitchen equipment in Sheffield in northern England in the 1970s felt that she had come up with an unambiguous marker of class, which most middle class kitchens contained, but was absent from all working class households and this was the garlic crusher. One simple, but significant, object appeared to crystallize a whole bundle of social, cultural, and economic attributes, concentrating them to a single point. Whether if the survey was repeated 30 years later the same would be true is not clear – tastes have changed and greater travel and exposure to other cuisines have altered what people eat. Sheffield has a large south Asian population, but few migrants from the Mediterranean. In Melbourne (supposedly the third largest Greek city in the world) or New York the garlic crusher would be found more evenly spread across the city and other markers of class would have to be sought.

Each of us has a mix of possessions which are diagnostic of class differences in the area we live (type of house, furnishing, books, music, forms of socializing) causing us to think how might these provide different insights from evidence of income, occupation, and tastes, compared with the results of an interview.

Chapter 6
The prehistory of the future

Prehistory is alive and well, inhabiting the area of our lives least easily put into words: our connection to material things. Many of our most significant others are not people, but objects; and especially significant objects are not strangers to us, they are known, loved, and lived with. Cooking utensils, cars, beds, computers, hammers, or pens each hold a set of possibilities within, immediately apparent to those who know them well. Prehistory is less a period and more a set of potentialities which we know, sense, and feel, but find hard to speak. Realizing the potentials of the material world lies at the heart of what makes us, and has made us, human. It is a thread to follow into the silent parts of the human story. To attune ourselves to prehistory, past and present, we need to resonate with the non-verbal bits of human experience. I am aware of the irony of writing to say that words are only part of our story.

Crucially for the prehistory of the present, the world is being reconfigured, profoundly changing our relations with material things. A new type of space has emerged, changing what we do day to day and creating new mythologies: cyberspace. This is a term coined by the writer William Gibson in his novel *Neuromancer* to describe the new mass of interconnections between people, machines, and information which Gibson calls a 'consensual hallucination'. It makes no sense to ask 'Where is cyberspace?', despite the spatial metaphor. It is virtual, that is to say notional, imagined, not concrete or really real. But, of course, it does exist as a set of connections and relations between hardware, software, and wetware (that's us – the cyberliterature is replete with new terms).

One of the intellectual products of web connectedness has been a shift from an interest in entities to the defining of relationships. The 19th and earlier 20th centuries divided up the world in order to study it. The Linnean classification of biologists was copied in many areas of study. It was the ethnologist and archaeologist Pitt Rivers who coined the term 'typology', and types became basic to understanding regional and chronological differences, encoded in the periods of European prehistory: the Stone, the Bronze, and the Iron Ages. In order to make sense of a mass of diverse material it is useful to divide this into stone, bone, pot, and metal or to distinguish the Lower, Middle, and Upper Palaeolithic. Disciplines arose around these classifications, so that archaeology split off from ethnology, and first museums, then academic departments, gave institutional structure to these classifications. Now we have many specialists – those who look at Neolithic pots, but know little of Iron Age ceramics; people who know about the prehistory of coastal New Guinea, but not the Highlands of that country. These divisions and specialisms have been most productive, but they do divide.

What was put asunder is now being recombined. Disciplinary boundaries are breaking down, so that the study of material culture can be carried out by prehistorians, historians, anthropologists, or geographers. Prehistorians studying material culture are wary of their own classifications, wondering how much sense it makes always to separate the study of pottery from that of metalwork or basketry, and are thinking of putting these pieces together in ways that provide a more holistic view of human social and sensory experience.

A stress on relations is unsurprising given the changes in how we live. In cyberspace relations work to change entities. Multiple User Domains (MUDs) are groups into which people can enter as themselves or someone of a different gender or even species. New identities are not adopted randomly, but help people work through issues in the rest of their lives. A woman who lost a leg in an accident developed a one-legged MUD persona who had a series of satisfying virtual relationships, opening up the possibility of real-life relationships. MUDs have become rich areas of anthropological study. Predictably perhaps, despite the unfettered possibilities of virtual inventiveness, many new personae are depressingly familiar; a 'Boy's Own' mentality has dominated much of the new culture.

Nevertheless, entities are up for grabs, reworked through new virtual relations, leading to a greater fluidity in the realm of ideas. Entities are under threat from other elements of cyberculture, such as the notion of the cyborg. Part-person, part-machine, the cyborg belongs to a science-fiction future. Or does it? Many would argue that we are all already cyborgs. Medical interventions have changed our biochemistry through inoculations or even created people through IVF. Our organs can be removed or replaced and machinery introduced into the body in the form of a pacemaker or new hip joint. The distinctions between person and object will blur further over the next few years. Many of us are linked to machines for long stretches of the day. Cars, computers, telephones, industrial machinery, and the TV all have fundamental effects on our bodies, thoughts, and feelings. No wonder that many studying material culture are unhappy with the subject–object distinction. The changing world of the present has caused many prehistorians to think about our past differently, searching out the intimate connections that have always existed between people and things. The study of the past and our understanding of the present are deeply entangled.

Cyberspace is infinitely complex and inter-connected; cyborgs are neither one thing nor the other. Academia is now tending to stress a lack of clear boundaries between both disciplines and objects of study, as well as non-linear movements of history, thought, and action. The onwards and upwards progressive histories of the

Victorians are gradually being replaced with views that stress the complexity of history and not its directional nature. Many areas of the world have rejected the Three Age system of Stone, Bronze, and Iron, a rejection increasingly appealing to many in Europe.

Cyberspace is still very new, but not unprecedented. As a virtual system it stands as the latest in a long line of such systems, the most influential of which is language. Fully modern humans have been speaking for at least the last 40,000 years. Much of this conversation has probably been gossip, just as ours is in the present. Whether Neanderthals or even earlier ancestors could speak is still debated, as they may not have possessed the right architecture of mouth and throat to produce the same subtle range of sounds we do. Whether they were capable of humour, irony, fantasy, and myth we will probably never know. We do have one big clue to the development of language. Around 40,000 years ago there is a huge upsurge in symbolism, through rock art, carved animal and human figures, and decoration on objects.

The classic definition of a symbol is 'something that stands for something else' – the colour red for blood, which then might be generalized as a symbol for danger. In his book *The Prehistory of Mind* Steven Mithen sees a shift from human ancestors, up to and including the Neanderthals, who had a number of domain-specific intelligences, each concerning technology, the natural world, and the social world. They were unable to connect these different domains of thought. If Mithen is correct then the Boxgrove hominids, with whom I started this book, could think about the behaviour of horses with one part of their mind, making a handaxe with another, and their own position within the group using a third. They could not connect these areas of thought in any effective manner. The last 40,000 years has seen the rise of what Mithen terms 'cognitive fluidity', which can make connections between the natural and social worlds. Contemporary hunter-gatherers might see an animal as their ancestor, which must be treated with respect when killed and eaten. Such connections were impossible for the

Boxgrove hominids, he argues. The basis of cognitive fluidity is the ability to create symbols. When something can be seen to stand for something else all sorts of connections become possible, so that the separateness of domain-specific intelligences breaks down.

I take a rather different view of intelligence to Mithen, seeing it as a quality of our bodies as much as our minds. Working intelligently on and in the world our ancestors seamlessly combined the social and the natural. If the Boxgrove hominids did hunt, then this required a sophisticated understanding of animal behaviour and coordinated social action. Dividing culture and nature as separate categories of thought as Mithen does only occurred in the last few hundred years. However, what was only incipient prior to 40,000 years ago was the tension between the virtual world of words and the concrete realm of actions and relationships. A key element of modern human behaviour is that we can do things, but we can also think about doing things. Until sophisticated forms of symbolism developed 40,000 years ago, there were few symbolic means of constructing the world of action, so that hominids were more bound up in the immediacy of their material and sensory worlds. Symbolic forms of speech and representation operate through links to the world (blood⇒red⇒danger), but over time they also develop their own internal logics, which make these links much less straightforward. Sahlins's telling of the death of Cook pointed out that Hawaiians and Europeans worked with their own sets of cultural logics; their actions were motivated by one set of events, but also by the different sense they both made of those events. Modern human action and intelligence came about not through linking domains of thought previously separate, as Mithen has argued, but through setting up a tension between action and thought. Thought, in turn, is possible through symbolism which can recreate the everyday world in virtual form. The digital words I am creating now will be transferred later to the page to evoke (I hope) thoughts and feelings on the part of you the reader. Words are not the world itself, but do stand in a complex relationship to the world.

The virtual world, which was first brought into existence by sophisticated symbolic language, is in tension with the practical world, but is not totally opposed to it. As Renfrew has pointed out, a concept of weight is hard to conceive of in the absence of some material set of weights and could not have arisen purely as an idea. Now that they do exist as concepts measures of weight can be added or subtracted arithmetically and treated in a manner quite divorced from actual weights. Weight is both a concept and an actuality, virtual and real.

Cyberspace is a virtual system of relations that could not exist without computers, Ethernet cables, and people at keyboards. It exists both in our heads and at our fingertips. Cyberspace has created its own mythologies, gripping our imagination, as shown by increasing numbers of books and films featuring the net, helping to dispel one myth that we live by – that we have no myths. Prehistoric relations between people and pots or pots and metal vessels hold no straightforward guides to present cyber and cyborg culture. But the tension between the material and the virtual has existed for at least the last 40 millennia and there are lessons to be learnt today from long-term relationships and tensions.

The present world is changing fast, giving new shape to old relations. We are uncertain of who we are, as part-people and part-objects, or of where we are going as a non-linear future unfolds. Oscar Wilde said that our one duty to history is to rewrite it. We have a growing sense that history is rewriting us.

Further reading

Chapter 1

B. Connolly and R. Anderson, *First Contact* (Viking Penguin, 1987):
how prehistory ended in the New Guinea Highlands.

C. Gamble, *The Palaeolithic Societies of Europe* (Cambridge University
Press, 1999): an intelligent and detailed account of the earliest
prehistory of Europe.

Ongka, *Ongka: A Self-Account by a New Guinea Big-Man*, trans.
A. Strathern (Duckworth, 1979).

M. Pitts and M. Roberts, *Fairweather Eden* (Century, 1997): an
excellent account of the work, personalities and findings at Boxgrove.

J. N. Postgate, *Early Mesopotamia: Society and Economy at the Dawn of
History* (Routledge, 1994): good background of the origins of writing
in Mesopotamia and Mesopotamian influences elsewhere.

Chapter 2

R. Dunbar, *Gossip, Grooming and the Evolution of Language*
(Faber, 1997): discusses the links between brain size and social
complexity in primates and the origins of language in humans.

C. Gamble, *Timewalkers: The Prehistory of Global Colonization*
(Penguin, 1993).

M. Mauss, *The Gift*, trans. W. D. Halls (Routledge, 1990, 1st published
1928): a classic work of French anthropology that laid much of the
basis for understanding exchange and social relations in kin-based
societies.

Chapter 3

R. Gould and M. Schiffer (eds.), *Modern Material Culture: The Archaeology of Us* (Academic Press, 1981): has a lively chapter by Rathje on the Tucson Garbage Project, plus other interesting material.

T. Ingold, *The Perception of the Environment* (Routledge, 2000): excellent on hunter-gatherer relationships with their landscapes.

G. Stocking, *Victorian Anthropology* (Free Press, 1987): dense, but excellent account of the debates of the nineteenth century and their social context.

B. Trigger, *A History of Archaeological Thought* (Cambridge University Press, 1989): the most comprehensive account there is.

Chapter 4

P. Bogucki, *The Origins of Human Society* (Blackwell, 1999): a well-written and comprehensive account of human prehistory, developed around a notion of progress.

Y. Bonnefoy (ed.), *Mythologies*, trans. W. Donniger (Chicago University Press, 1991): a comprehensive survey, originally in French, of world mythologies.

V. G. Childe, *What Happened in History* (Penguin, 1942): classic account of human history by the most influential archaeologist of the earlier 20th century.

J. Diamond, *Guns, Germs and Steel* (Vintage, 1998): a lively and provocative account of human history from an evolutionary perspective.

S. Fiedel, *Prehistory of the Americas* (Cambridge University Press, 1992).

A. Moore, G. Hillman, and A. Legge, *Village on the Euphrates* (Oxford University Press, 2000): the site report on Abu Hureyra – large but worth the effort.

C. Renfrew, *Archaeology and Language* (Jonathan Cape, 1987): this book rekindled archaeologists' interests in the history of languages and put forward the hypothesis that the spread of the major language families was due to the movements of farmers.

—— and K. Boyle (eds.), *Archaeogenetics: DNA and the population prehistory of Europe* (McDonald Institute for Archaeological Research, 2000): explores the possibility of a 'grand synthesis' of archaeological genetic and linguistic data, focusing on the new genetic information.

T. Shaw, P. Sinclair, B. Andah, and A. Okpoko (eds.), *The Archaeology of Africa* (Routledge, 1993).

A. Sherratt, *Economy and Society in Prehistoric Europe* (Princeton University Press, 1997): an account of European prehistory that tries to develop an holistic and materialist perspective.

Chapter 5

R. Gilchrist, *Gender and Archaeology* (Routledge, 1999): contains a comprehensive overview of the issues surrounding gender, worked through a number of case studies.

C. Gosden, *Anthropology and Archaeology* (Routledge, 1999): looks at questions of aesthetics and transformations as approached from both an archaeological and anthropological perspective.

—— (ed.), *Archaeology and Aesthetics, World Archaeology*, 33 (2001).

P. Kirch, *On the Road of the Winds* (University of California Press, 2002): a comprehensive and accessible account of Pacific prehistory.

G. Lock, C. Gosden, D. Miles, and S. Palmer, *Uffington White Horse Hill and its Landscape* (Oxford Committee for Archaeology, in press).

M. Sahlins, *Islands of History* (University of Chicago Press, 1985): a difficult but fascinating account of Pacific history, including the death of Cook.

Chapter 6

D. Bell and B. Kennedy (eds.), *The Cybercultures Reader* (Routledge, 2000).

S. Mithen, *The Prehistory of the Mind* (Thames & Hudson, 1996): emphasizes the importance of mind rather than bodily intelligence, but provides a lively and interesting account of this important subject.

T. Taylor, *The Prehistory of Sex* (Fourth Estate, 1996): lively but generally uncritical survey of a subject bound to sell books.

Timelines

Africa

*c.*120,000 BC	First fully modern humans (in a physical, if not behavioural, sense)
120,000	Klasies River Mouth site: evidence of fishing, shellfish gathering, and seabird predation; fishhooks and stone tools
*c.*100,000	First movement of fully modern humans out of Africa
40,000	Beginning of the Late Stone Age (LSA); human adornment in form of ostrich eggshell beads
30,000	Southern African rock art; possible development of the bow and arrow
6000	Cattle pastoralism in north Africa; settled agriculture in Egypt
5000	Sorghum, African rice, and guinea fowl all domesticated in the circum-Saharan area by this date
4000–3000	Development of hieroglyphic script in Egypt; end of prehistory there
3000–2000	By this time cattle and goats introduced into sub-Saharan Africa (quite possibly earlier); African yams and oil palm domesticated; dates of tea and coffee unknown

800	Copper working in West Africa (may date earlier)
500	Evidence of iron smelting in Nigeria and central Niger; spreads to rest of West Africa by AD 1000
0	Spread of cattle, sheep, and iron to southern Africa

Americas

South

13,000 BC	Monte Verde
12,000	Clovis
6000	Potatoes, maize, beans in the Andes
5000	Pottery in the Amazon and Andes
3500	Pots, cotton, and domesticated camelids, guinea pigs, in the Andes
900	Large ceremonial centres in the Andes
AD 100	Rise of Tiwanku polities, ultimate ancestors of Inca empire

Central

12,000	Clovis
7000	First squash and gourds
5000	Maize and beans
2500	Pottery
1000	Earliest state formation
500	Writing in the Mayan area
AD 1000	Metal production

North

12,000	Clovis
10,000	Folsom
7000	Gourds and squash in the Mid-West
4000	Pottery and copper in the Mid-West
3000	Maize in the South-West

2000	Bow and arrow in the Arctic
1000	Pottery in the Arctic and South-West
600	Pottery and maize in Great Basin

Asia

South-West

15,000 BC	Expansion out of refugia?
12,000	Natufian
10,000	Pre-pottery Neolithic; earliest cereal and animal domestication
9500	Start of Abu Hureyra
6500	Hassuna and Samarran painted pots, baskets, obsidian, copper beads, olives, and vines
5000	Tripartite houses; ploughs
4000	Wheel-turned pottery
3500	Cities in Mesopotamia; first bronze working and writing

Central and East

7000	Farming villages from Turkmenistan to Baluchistan: domesticated cereals and animals
6500	Rice cultivation, pottery, and villages in China
3000	Bronze and silk weaving in China; rice in Thailand and Vietnam
2500	Cities in the Indus Valley
1800	Start of Shang dynasty, China
1400	First Chinese writing

Australia and the Pacific

40,000+ BC	First colonization
35,000	First island colonization: New Ireland
30,000	First rock art: Australia; first colonization of the Solomon Islands
25,000	First occupation of Australian central desert
20,000	Movement of obsidian and animals in New Guinea
14,000?	First use of tree crops: New Guinea
8000	Sea level rise divides Australia and New Guinea
6000	First horticultural systems in Highland New Guinea; dog introduced in Australia; new tool types in Australia
3500	Lapita expansion into the Pacific as far as Tonga and Samoa
1000	Sweet potato introduced into Pacific from South America
AD 1000	Sedentary settlement on Murray River, Australia; first settlement of Hawai'i, Easter Island, and New Zealand
1350	Sweet potato introduced into New Guinea Highlands
1788	First white settlement of Australia

Europe

c.40,000 BC	First fully modern humans
15,000	Expansion out of refugia in Iberia–Southern France, Balkans–Ukraine
10,000	Wild grains, fruit, and marine resources utilized
6500	Early Neolithic villages in south-east Europe; cereals and domesticated animals
4500	Earliest use of copper

4000	First farming in north-west and first megaliths
3500	Ploughs and carts
3000	Wool and horses
2000	First texts in Minoan palaces
2300	First use of bronze
800	Introduction of iron; urbanization in Mediterranean
100	First urban settlements in northern Europe

Index

Prehistory

Visit the
VERY SHORT INTRODUCTIONS
Web site

www.oup.co.uk/vsi

➤ **Information** about all published titles

➤ News of **forthcoming books**

➤ **Extracts** from the books, including titles not yet published

➤ **Reviews** and views

➤ **Links** to other **web sites** and main OUP web page

➤ Information about **VSIs in translation**

➤ **Contact** the editors

➤ **Order** other **VSIs** on-line

Expand your collection of
VERY SHORT INTRODUCTIONS

SOCIAL AND CULTURAL ANTHROPOLOGY
A Very Short Introduction

John Monaghan and Peter Just

'If you want to know what anthropology *is*, look at what anthropologists *do*.'

This Very Short Introduction to Social and Cultural Anthropology combines an accessible account of some of the discipline's guiding principles and methodology with abundant examples and illustrations of anthropologists at work.

Peter Just and John Monaghan begin by discussing anthropology's most important contributions to modern thought: its investigation of culture as a distinctly 'human' characteristic, its doctrine of cultural relativism, and its methodology of fieldwork and ethnography. They then examine specific ways in which social and cultural anthropology have advanced our understanding of human society and culture, drawing on examples from their own fieldwork. The book ends with an assessment of anthropology's present position, and a look forward to its likely future.

www.oup.co.uk/vsi/anthropology